# WORLD ABSOLUTE THEORY

## THE LIFE AND DEATH OF HUMAN CIVILIZATION

MOHAMMAD YOUNUS

Copyright © Mohammad Younus
All Rights Reserved.

This book has been self-published with all reasonable efforts taken to make the material error-free by the author. No part of this book shall be used, reproduced in any manner whatsoever without written permission from the author, except in the case of brief quotations embodied in critical articles and reviews.

The Author of this book is solely responsible and liable for its content including but not limited to the views, representations, descriptions, statements, information, opinions and references ["Content"]. The Content of this book shall not constitute or be construed or deemed to reflect the opinion or expression of the Publisher or Editor. Neither the Publisher nor Editor endorse or approve the Content of this book or guarantee the reliability, accuracy or completeness of the Content published herein and do not make any representations or warranties of any kind, express or implied, including but not limited to the implied warranties of merchantability, fitness for a particular purpose. The Publisher and Editor shall not be liable whatsoever for any errors, omissions, whether such errors or omissions result from negligence, accident, or any other cause or claims for loss or damages of any kind, including without limitation, indirect or consequential loss or damage arising out of use, inability to use, or about the reliability, accuracy or sufficiency of the information contained in this book.

Made with ♥ on the Notion Press Platform
www.notionpress.com

# Contents

| | |
|---|---|
| *Preface* | *v* |
| *Author's Word* | *vii* |
| 1. Concept Of Law And Twenty-first Century | 1 |
| 2. Un Sovereignty: Transformation For This Age [international Organizations (io)] | 44 |
| 3. Ideas Of Politics: Socrates And Prophet Muhammad | 81 |

# Preface

The sole power of human is- 'words' (includes all expressions), human can only think and speak or express, a person tries to express and achieve the results but there is no guarantees of consequences. It is the world's nature that here only can think and speak, there is no guarantee of anything. The 'words' is the ultimate tools for all, and then try but no guarantee of any results. Even God sent the prophets only deliver 'words', their only job was to speak. The creation of civilization is through words, advocacy. This is an effort based world, not result based.

The creation of civilization is through words, through advocacy. The name of the most powerful weapon in this changed world, in the eternal duality of truth and falsehood, is - 'word'; its best and maximum use will determine which way the world will go. The present world is called the 'War of Words', the world of words, the world of information or media. Silence is not a good sign in this world, is not always a sign of wisdom. 'Silence' is enough for the destruction of mankind, only the dawn light of the terrible night that is descending to extinguish the light of mankind. So, turn on the light, clear light...

There is one powerful and absolute thing that no one or nothing can possess or control until the owner allows and that is- human brain. Everything good or bad starts- process- originated from there. This is the absolute human power and potentials that limitless and exclusive. The best and fundamental communication mode of brain is- word, it works efficient and can come out with a better outcome. Without word, other languages it never recognized and respond rightly. The words are the most valuable and

# PREFACE

ultimate human power or potentials.

The politics, law and organizations are the greatest and fundamental developments of the human civilizations that connect- communicate- educate people. These are the necessary and most effective human developed system to deal with human issues. The foundation of these 3 historical landmark developments are the – words, the two use of words- to express [communicate] and to write [document]. These are the best utilization platforms of the words, the best results can be made there for the mankind. By the time, some extreme, improper and immature deviations happen, it should be addressed soon.

"The best use of word can change the world."

# Author's Word

This book can be titled 'A Common Man's word' or 'You can think like the way' or 'You can see like the way'. The book has just shared a different perspective or outlook. This book is not offering any solution, neither accepting nor rejecting any solution or system. It may be a single dot with others or may not be. It may support the world to think, think wisely and necessarily which may support human civilization to make it better or may not.

It is not fiction or any form of literature, not any grammatical textbook or creative writing course book, not any research or research methodology text book, it is not teaching material and it is conscious decision. It is a book of philosophy, philosophy of 3 most powerful and ruling systems of the human civilization, with philosophy in each word.

**For any queries: younus.words@gmail.com**

# CHAPTER I

# Concept of Law and Twenty-First Century

The world goals should be lawless (ultimate peace, just and civilised but dictionary defined the term wrongly and ignorantly), not lawness. Extremely obsessive or addicted to law is lawness, kill the human conscience and dignity in place of law is lawness, without diagnosing problem properly enacting law constant- infinite is lawness. Lawness is to think law is the alone- independent solution of all problems, builds law such powerful than human dignity and necessity, to make the world rough or messy through ineffective and scattered countless law. Law-courts- prison is opium today, drink it and peace; it is no more question of good- fit or not. Here law represents or constitutes human brain manipulation mechanism for time, defocus root causes, weapon of injustice.

Human made the law for own necessity, it comes from culture- custom- religion etc. Law is just a framed document of human practice of this area, collection of some principles, human enact or framed it as document for good governance as supporting entity. Human are the leaders of the world, if citizen decided today they run the state without any framed law and no law would exist, human have that ability or freedom. There law is truly a great invention, civilizing force.

When law develops greater than human beings, law becomes king and punishing tools, human beings submit their conscience to law and addict to law where law becomes a place of faith than faith on human beings, losing faith on human beings in place of law constant, then law is in question. There law is the greatest insulting invention to the human civilization, the opium manipulate human brain, a dangerous weapon to crime and injustice. Consequently, law and human beings stand face to face, law and society confronted, not in way of friendship and solution rather hostility and problems. Excess or exceed of ability is dangerous. Today, there is no single sphere where law does not exist but problems everywhere and increasing at a higher rate.

There is a matter of regrets that a world or state ignorance about human potential and keep losing faith on human beings insensitively or negligibly, cannot think without law, cannot find any alternative except punishment and killing citizen, not go for root causes for sustainable solution rather on instant- populist- temporary destructive moves, people addicts and leaders of the people tricks to defocus root cause by enacting a last minute emergency regular legislation.

The world believes that by whom this world-civilization- society, to kill them is solution, not take or walk with them. So, human beings are today killing each other to vanish themselves. This is a world of prison-courts- law, not world of mankind. Law possessed and leads or control humans intelligence who made the law and it dies. It is like that not fear of artificial intelligence think like human, fear about human think and acts like artificial intelligence. Humans are mostly in race- competition- fight for living, cannot have time to think, such world humans itself made today. But, human must stop and think today, where they are and what they are doing, why?

What is law, what should be law, what extent law to? This longstanding question should be addressed on the context of 21$^{st}$ century as much as possible. It is we the people decide about the world, peoples are the leaders of the world. If want to see a better world, must stop and think, find the root cause and proceed. There is a country lots of law and it increase, increasing courts and prison which is inadequate to deal with that much cases, is it a great country? Or law does not require, prison closing daily, courts passing lazy time for no cases, is it a great country?

Law can never control human being, can support, there is nothing in this world can control human being. The serious problem is today, world tries to find all the solution in law, enacting law and increasing extreme to extreme punishment but why a person doing crime after knowing its punishment? Law does not have or find this answer of the question. The world decides today that without force- fear- punishment human can never be corrected, humans are bad in nature. If label or branded someone like this, there lose the opportunity to address the root cause of the issues.

The greatest failure of the human civilization that cannot protect, preserve and respect or understand human dignity, conscience and self- respect that creates a sense of understanding and practice where law dies. It is a failure that cannot build such system or environment where can say humans are civilized, there law is unnecessary, full faith on human beings.

There constantly creates problem and with enacting more and more law, no one stop here and solve. Everyday punishment- fear increased, human's area limits and binds, human potential suppressed.

WORDS: THE ABSOLUTE THEORY

The world think about visible success of few, the world does not have the ability to count how brilliant mind killed by the law and brand them criminal, they were potential human being. A killing mission with law world takes, there is neither place of understanding nor correcting. This law and courts punished and killed the "Socrates", today same legal system continued but no one concerned though celebrate Socrates all. It also allows to war and kill the innocent people. The world today in hectic to kill human being named or branded in different names and there intake everyday's law certify it is good or right. The law decides or allows to kill human being, if decision proves wrong, then law does not face nothing, no answer. This world branded people bad and kill, enact laws to certify or purify this to right. There is a deep rooted war today between law and human beings, law and mankind. This brainless or dumb law enacts, people submit and trial with psychological bias to kill and punishment, decreed to kill people thousands.

Human beings kill human beings and laughing at success, the President of a state delivering success stories that he/she chained or prisoned or killed more of his/her citizen in this year. To obey someone as judge or to make someone judge is the another grievous insult to the human ability and dignity. How can someone equal- same human being- judging other?! This court is the another sign of insulting human dignity. It is a matter of true surprise that made such world where one commits wrong to another and make judge a third. The fact is in most of the countries feels the courts and judges are too inadequate as cases are much as burden that creates serious backlog or tangle. Here demands to increase budget and establish more courts and more judges and more prison.

4

There increasing of law with punishment- courts- prison and budget on that is dangerous, alarming and greatest failure that does not create any sense or touched or connects to human mind. Insensibly, increase law-courts- prison, it does not alarm on mind, feel as it common; not any thoughts to decrease it, limits it and humanize it, then it must predictable that the results in disaster or destruction. It is established fact that nothing can control human beings except oneself and there though this legal system operates in every place but crimes constantly challenge the system and proves it wrong that crime commits increasingly. The whole legal system and concepts or thoughts build on it complete in question today.

It is a great failure of a country that the country failed to stop crime and build a civilized society, but chained the citizen in prison or jail, kill them. To sent jail or execute more capital punishment of own citizen is not a matter of proud or success and laugh, rather state should feel ashamed- regrets- concern and government should not sleep at night. It is great failure of a world that the world failed to resolve a global concern sustainably- peacefully, but declare war or use force against weak or same human being and kill thousands of people, later proves own fault and just say sorry as such Iraq war.

There is no point of immediate close or abolish the present legal system, the question is on increasing rate and race of law- punishment without addressing root causes, insensibly loosing faith on human beings and submit to law- punishment, the question is about reformation of not only system but also thoughts and ideas with system. A positive- better- true or clear sense and understanding -target or ultimate goals- thoughts and concept should must have, no error in aims at least.

The crisis is law is not human needs today, human lives in lawness world today. Law becomes human brain manipulation mechanism as fear as psychological bias to force- instant populist solution- defocus root causes-weapon of injustice by politicians. Law is not for human beings today, it only kills and punish human beings, branded human beings bad- brutish- criminal in nature. Increasing prison- law- courts and judges is not the success of a country, success is decreasing all of these.

There is no alternative to believe on human beings, the world is about human and it is humans world, to kill or prisoned them is not never a sustainable solution of any issues, killing people- then world for what and whom, if killing or vanish human beings- so work or betterment for whom, who are there to work.

It is human's world, there everything moves with human, without human beings this world is others. In humans world, whatever the ways, it must be with human, by killing people or losing faith on human is nothing to achieve, when job is to betterment for mankind then how lose faith on human? If lose faith on mankind, how proceed for them, connect with them and address the issues sustainably!

So, there must keep faith on human being, according to full respect to human dignity takes any step. If human does not understand or feel or want, there is no force can bound or control human, they revolt in different manners. Therefore, to punish or kill someone is not rather go in deep root causes and try to understand or connect, takes time and proceed for necessary- effective- sustainable solution. Law may acts as supporting entity but it should not be defocusing root cause or instigate for instant temporary solution. The other fundamental organs of governance must operate proper, efficiently and necessarily. Where punishment should be last, it is today first and foremost. The world goals should be kill the laws, decreasing and innecessiate laws, creates lawless world.

Law is the common sense, law comes from conscience, when conscience lost or died, law does not have any real existence, has lost its value completely which carried today. When law judge its origin as poor- bad- brutish, kill common sense and conscience- negligibly makes it ineffective and unnecessary, then law lost own applicability and ignorantly becomes more and more harsh but problems become uncontrolled as origin of the law died, law can't stand in any case rather constantly revealed and grow its limitations.

Human never be forced, they will revolt.

Law should not be created a negative- barbaric- ultravirus environment which even law's out of control. Law never an independent solution, should not ask all the solution from law. Law should not be tools to defocus root causes, instrument of strategical injustice, defocus governance necessity. We fed and empower much that becomes Frankenstein which uncontrollable itself and to us also. We made the law, if problem within us, if we are not aware or concern, how law can solve it which made by us?! We must concern and solve it first as good governance ourselves, we must address root causes, law may act as supporting entity always.

It is impossible that law gives all the solutions, law control its origin and establish peace, law is not such framework ever, though it just a framed document of human practice or common good but today develops a dangerous psychological biasness to law to ask or demands solution of any or all the issues and enactment to satisfy to

WORDS: THE ABSOLUTE THEORY

defocus root causes.

Without proper understanding about human nature, human potentials, a human beings, any kind of framework would go in vain. The world runs under humans decision-human thoughts, confront with human nature it is impossible to exist where human are the leaders, there law doing things to label them bad in nature who develops this world as modern as civilized today. That is why today law exists only in paper, there is no applicability of it because it cannot get human acceptance, in human's world without human acceptance nothing can be worked properly.

The world should be, it must be set goal on conscience based world- common sense based world- human-centric world, law always should a optional- supporting- limited necessity or entity. Nothing should be greater than own or human, human should not lost in any tools which they invent, human should never be jailed in humans world, believe on human that human cannot be bad. Everything shall be respectful to human limitless equal inherent potentials and human dignity. If human lost in human's world, the world only have the way to destroy. A car should never used its full speed and never in such speed that driver and car both failed to control, lost control over and just stopped in a destructive accident. This is human's world, what kind of world they want to see and what ability they have, they should decide. There is no one or nothing to interfere, it is humans world, the governance on humans.

There law failed to do something, but it goes extreme to extreme punishment and its rudeness- roughness increased. Law is unable to serve food but law prisoned in rigorous and it increased in extreme. In one side, something failed but shows arrogance of ignorance. Law mostly failed to control situation or gets acceptance of

8

human being as it passed without proper understanding root cause and human beings, law negativise and branded people bad. On the development of civilization law should be updated and owes positive impact on the modern days, but law rather return back to extreme to extreme barbaric age and barbaric framework. The world ahead's but laws go back in barbaric age to more continuously. If the world needs such law, how can say it is modern day or civilized world?! If it is not civilized, humans are not civilized or educated properly, uncivilized law cannot contribute there rather find the root cause and frame the theory to develop minds or humans, fulfil necessity, creates a good environment to deal with.

To kill- hit- fear- force- prison cannot make any sustainable solution, human must deliberately accept the truth. If problems in human, solve in it first, instant punishing decrees does not ensure anything rather messed much. If it is civilized era than other ages, accordingly law must also be civilized- develop and adapt in civilization of today.

If problems increasing with progress or development, and in keeping with that increasing more extreme laws does not make any better outcome, because problems in development concept or ways and diagnosing problems properly is must to reach in a sustainable solution. For all the problems or any issues, just enactment of law is not the solution or close the problems permanently, it may support but not resolved.

If problems and solution does not connect, the issues never be resolved. It is a matter of regrets that today just try to hide the real problems at any way like emergency extreme legislation, not go in deep root causes. As a result, progress comes scatteredly but peace is not. With progress some challenges comes but without proper diagnosing uncountable extreme law enacts, challenges going rough than anytime. The limitations of law must be understood and law must live in its space. Law should not be a fire on blind hand, instant populist magic, place of independent solution framework. Without addressing root cause of the crisis, only enacting more and more psychologically bias and human disgracing laws can never give a sustainable solution of the crisis. Rather it creates more problems oriented- intolerant- dehumanize environment, confronting human nature where human becomes uncontrolled. Ultimate this dictating- fearing- manipulating laws are surrendered, it is humans world and human made this world but the way not been stopped yet, it again repeats in a way which creates much dangerous crisis and loss of human.

So, the law should not consider what law is not or what law cannot be, law has its own ability and instinct. Law act as supporting entity with other fundamental solution mechanism i.e. government and must address the root cause. The instant- temporary- magical solution in rat race creates crisis more dangerous as uncontrollable. For a better world human must stop and think.

Mankind invented destructive weapon for the world, but cannot invented still any protective weapon. Weapon cannot protects or stops weapon, its only destroy something to someone. Man made human killing laws, they cannot made laws for life. People have death today, not life.

The relations between law and humans are complete opposite or extremely dialectical though law born for human and human made law. Either human beings feared law or breaks and revolt to the law, law severely failed to connect people. Law became a fearing- forcing- punishing mechanism and a negative or bad or disturbing things to the people. In some minor cases people may follows the law as binding as imposing but the deliberate acceptance of law in majority cases is so poor. People disturbed and disgraced by this punishing law, they feared and fleeing from that or breaks it as revolt.

The extreme punishment lost the importance of law in actual, people habituated and does not care or touched by it. There extreme to extreme punishment have been passed but crime never been stopped where punishment becomes a funny tales today. The constant failure of punishment or scattered force made law valueless and misfit. Furthermore, the punishing law in most cases misused according to available reports in many countries, false case and harassment alarmingly it increased but no peace and justice it ensured sustainably.

The ultimate aims of law is to establish peace and justice is devastating though law and punishment available and increasing. Law dehumanize the circumstances- negativise peoples mind- creates more serious crime as ordinary. Law confronts human nature, and human creates better way to do crime and proves law failed. Law try to impose or enforce, law made or treat people as slave, law defines people beast- animal [Father of Law- Thomas Hobbes], and today they cannot think human beings are human actually, lost the own identity; the law not stops but continues with an wrong- rough- unnatural mind in that modern era to destroy or buried mankind in complete. Law just became or acts as a tools to brand people bad, labelled people brutish in that modern civilization. Law divides people, failed unites. It kills humanity- empathy- natural order, law creates negativity- suspicion- dishonour to mankind which destroy faith- relations- positivity. Law busy to chain and

## WORDS: THE ABSOLUTE THEORY

shut the people, peoples potentials and freedom, world busy to also shut own under barbed wire. Today world try to flee from the world, such extreme and uncontrollable crisis it creates. The relations- connections- acceptance of law to the public is extremely poor, it just a machine to brand people bad in nature and punished. The world developed, new civilizations modernize but law is in primitive- barbaric era.

Law enacted through few number of person named representatives, in national cases also public welfare and opinion does not considered rightly, the law passed to impose own thoughts- ideas of some group- ideology of something but the nature and necessity of people- the deep upgraded societies necessity is today immaterial. Though public opinion is the important source of law but there today party majority in parliament passed law to serve own ideology or thoughts of some part. Where law is the demands of society, it will implement in society but it is not connect with public or society, then how a law be followed deliberately! There some fix ideas and thoughts, ideologies are primary consideration; the states or peoples necessity, human nature study in depth is immaterial. Consequently, people refused to follow this detached law and there the courts- police- prison seat and impose punishment to bound or force or killing and labelled as bad in nature as criminal human beings that today such environment creates where human fear human- human hostile to human- world fleeing from own and confront each other to ensure or celebrate a historic destruction.

It is impossible to make a law efficient to confront nature, nature is the absolute, it must be respected nature. The law for human, human made the law, if the law does not understand human or human nature and it acts opposite, it can never be effective enactments. Today, the law enacted with complete opposite thoughts to human nature and when human refused to accept, then killed them, fall in race to increase extreme to extreme punishment and law without addressing the root causes, it is failed. As a result, there law and punishment increased as touch the sky, crimes are not stopped yet in a minimum rate rather alarmingly increased. Law completely disconnected with human nature- root causes, law builds the world more complex- fearing, law not made the world easy and better for the people. Law confronts with human nature and branded them- decide them bad in nature which wrong; it is made by today and to force- kill people to follow this kinds law, more and more controlling mechanism developed like CCTV, builds fearing- forcing- binding world.

The greatest failure of the law is – severely failed "to educate" people which is the main purpose of law. It creates fear- disgrace- hurts but completely failed to educate people. Education is not about fearing- forcing- hurting in that civilized age at least, it is about understanding- connecting- supporting. The extremely disgraceful punishing laws totally detached from that true way of law, it rather busier on killing- fearing- binding and instant closing the matters without addressing root causes. A killing- fearing- disgracing machine to the humanity never educate the human that already proved as common sense as it already branded human bad- brutish- criminal in nature which is seriously false. The ultimate purpose of law is to guide people in right way, educate them for better way, connect with laws framed civilized practices and builds a better society through law respecting human dignity, human nature.

Law guide and supports people for peace, for common good, law ensures justice and equality, it addresses root causes and develop a sustainable solution of the crisis. It is not the punishing- fearing- killing mechanism, instant on partial temporary decision is not law, law is not the enemy to the human. But, the world builds legal system that punishing- killing, confronting human nature, not addressing root causes. The punishment is the main focusing point of today's law and no concern about results of punishment, not guiding or educating people. Law comes from custom, law should develop a custom and people follows law like a custom in that civilized era but here it imposed or binds through punishment targetedly and constantly. It is impossible to educate people through a killing- punishing/fearing- disgracing law, without educating people law can never be establish any justice, peace or equality. The present law is not educating material at all, it is complete focus on just fear- punishment and labelled humans criminal or bad in nature. Law is the fearing tools, a disturbing- negative things to the people today, it is severely failed to connect and educate.

To educate- to connect- to aware people about something better principle and practices is the core purpose of law, through a follow-up mechanism it develops a customary system to the people respecting human dignity can be reached to the aims of the law that peace and justice [equitable rights ensure]. Law is not something fearing or negative, it is friends of people, it helps people to get better life, that understanding people should have. Where the issue is with people, there must connect people to resolve this sustainably. To build such environment or awareness about people's rights and duties concern, people's problems and solutions, peoples strength and weakness that leads a balanced- civilized- cooperative world with minimum/ controllable crimes. The law must find and educate people about root causes of the crisis, to build concern and share the best way to resolve equitably. Law educates people that people follow the law as custom and thousands of extreme controlling mechanism would be immaterial there. Law educate people to be human, law does not lies and labelled false as human bad in nature. Law shows the way, follow the way and builds the way respecting human nature and dignity.

It is matter of serious concerns that there thousands of law, increasing innumerable laws on the basis of false understanding and false mechanism targeted to kill and punish people. The existing system brands people criminal in nature constantly, it loses the opportunity to address the root causes and severely failed as detached from people. It increases more and more extreme punishment but it lost its value in ultimate. The law failed to serve its true purpose, it cannot be educated people rather it kills people or threats people. Consequently, there law is over than necessity, problems are not solved but increase and dangerous alarmingly as root causes are defocused and not addressed. The law aims at punishment, not educate; to force someone, not understand; to decide instant- partial, not root- complete. The result is law severely failed, human sufferings increased at an alarming rate, the world regular faces mysterious destructive accident and blame on different false area, a legislation may repeats again and on false foundation or understanding how much law can enact but no results come out at last, wrong is in root.

Everyday the world goes with severe loss, it is visible or invisible, individual or collective, reported or not. The peace or happiness is not there for long time, people only

WORDS: THE ABSOLUTE THEORY

struggle to live at any cost, nobody in happiness who has everything or who has nothing, nobody. Though this world and life is beautiful, world has available necessary resources than human needs, mankind are the leaders of the world but crimes- crisis- deaths leads the world today under human made suicidal system as human disgracing wrong killing legal system. All the human beings suffered seriously in different way for this root crisis knowingly or unknowingly.

The law labelled human rapist and killed but law failed to find root causes- original reasons- truth behind this-connects real facts, no reports- study- analysis in depth. There is no clear answer to law that why someone being rapist except some populist presumption, no regular research and study on that, why a human being raped- no one regrets but just killed and closed. Next day, more dangerous more rape incident occurred as without addressing root cause and proper study- understanding just kill and close to satisfy animality and wrong perception, law and punishment increased, and increased crime. The same thing happen that law labelled someone terrorist and so popular this today, it is popular- common phenomenon that no dialogue with terrorist or criminal, no study on rapist, just pass the law and killed- closed case. There is no deep concern and study of root causes of the issues that which entities or components connect and liable to happen this and why, no regrets that why someone being criminal like me, from same society I belong, why someone are criminals and why someone not, all are equal by birth; what is the root causes, what is the sustainable solution- never the thoughts and study peoples do or law address.

Law just labelled someone rapist or terrorist, and killed them but failed or unable to resolve the problems which repeats more in a dangerous way as the root cause has not been addressed. Law failed to educate and serve its true purpose, a government failed to provide a better life for its citizen but labelled people poor- bad- brutish (all the blame on public) and there no regrets- reports- reformation in root; law and government both togetherly or friendly just killed and labelled human as criminal as bad in nature, then pass more extreme punishing laws. World accepts or decides human beings are bad in nature, and no way. The result is the law and its acceptability extremely poor, it creates more dangerous- uncontrollable crime, an anarchist and dialectical system going on which alarmingly increases human sufferings in all over the world knowingly or unknowingly.

So, law severely failed in what the core job or purpose of law is, law mostly deviated from its core purpose or job what law can do, law deviated in a wrong way that with punishment- forceful mechanism to bound people to be the slave of law made under someone's fix thoughts or ideologies and impose it through law, law creates fear to make slave of some ideologies framed as law and people if refused it acts as killing machine, highly misused by different entities. There most of the law today extremely politicized and power based or influenced, minimum ethics even ignored today. The law by in nature it false, then it misused by powerful entities against one another which constitutes irreparable loss to the mankind that human kills human, the human war continuing long time under different wrong way where no one win but mankind devastatingly lose and suffered.

There is a surprising obsessiveness and advocacy of passing and following laws going on by academicians- politicians- judiciary but unfortunately there extreme inadequacy or shortage of research- reports- study on history and basis of existing legal system under modern or civilized age and human nature, the purpose and limitations of punishing law, the problems and necessary new developments of law, the foundation and philosophy of law on that very modern age etc. But, the advertisement and promotion they are doing to follow the law without check, be the slave of law without examine its foundation. There demands increases more and more extreme punishment and law on different deep issues but the proper study and understanding about punishment and its effectiveness or necessity regarding human nature is grossly absent. A race once start by someone, everyone just join and speed increasing but no one challenge or question or check on it, just it continues. Everyone's study partial inside of the law, no one see from the full or neutral outside and all searching solution inside tirelessly but no one tries come outside to see a neutral- necessary- complete picture from the irrespective of all above and find an true sustainable solution for the crisis.

Everyone sinked into law, no one think about law. The history, basic, concepts, development, modern age and human beings particularly regarding law is mostly out of concern but advertisements and enactments in different colour is extremely increased or continued. To examine the life and death of law is completely absent, the inside study or partial some analysis may there. It is a great concern for the law stakeholders that there understanding and analysis are in serious question that there extremely lacks the study on existing legal system and modern age, the birth of law and human nature, the constant failure of law and its root causes under existing legal system and civilized age. In case of, legal philosophy there rare development tough to find on the context of modern or civilized age [18th, 19th, 20th century].

With the comparison of development of pure science, the social science remarkable or mentionable developments are too few or tough to take or count name. The social sciences severely failed to balance with pure sciences, the incredible development of pure sciences possesses all the aspects in monopoly may though inability or failed to address by nature, social sciences existential resource are some old scattered developments.

The religion- philosophy- law [social sciences] just try to adjust and follow scientific development in that modern/ civilized age. The social sciences faces serious crisis of existence, an extreme imbalance, mostly it stuck into individual scattered practice under few older unauthenticated developments. Though this extreme imbalance creates crisis and question raise about scientific developments that its nature and ability. The scientific developments made huge- speedy progress in the human civilization, and the progress comes with different challenges. The culture- religion- ethics- laws etc. are the fundamental to human life, in extreme speed of materialistic progress under scientific development these philosophical or ethical parts of human life cannot properly developed which creates an imbalance- uncontrollable- extreme lifestyle of human being. There human beings faces different challenges to understand and choose the way, faces a serious dilemma, to adjust with high speed scientific progress different conceptual- philosophical- ethical gross gap creates. Theses gap should be covered, a balanced development inevitable between social and pure sciences both case for the better outcome.

There legal development is essential in accordance with scientific development and human nature study as it regulates people or state or whole world. Science already constantly proves that the basis of the existing legal system is completely wrong, human nature is- good or cooperative and philosophically it proves long ago. According to human nature and others different development the existing legal system and legal framework shall be developed necessarily as humans are the fundamental subjects of law. In that scientific era, it is clearly prove that physical presence does not matter but brain can do or operate anything from anywhere to everywhere, philosophically it also proves long time ago that crimes born in mind [mens rea]. The body is not material to the crime- to punish or prison or kill does not stop crime; it is about thought –ideology built in mind under many reasons or circumstances, so law must connect with thought- to educate people- to understand and find root causes to address. Without connecting in thought, fear- punishment- killing never stops crime which established fact that fear cannot clearly hear minds and the root cause must address together with good governance. Thought never dies, body may and government must address root cause with guiding law and principles together as any practical or real needs, deep rooted cultural issues etc. Fear never control human beings or impact on human mind positively, slavery is not human nature- it revolts. To resolve a human crisis, human must understand and must understand human, it must reach and understand the root cause.

Law alone is not independent solution mechanism, it is supporting entity, and punishment is not solution, it should never be targeted as goal. People must out from the illusion that law is the solution, it is a single step of solution, it may helps a bit but there some other entities exist with law to make a sustainable solution collectively. Law can educate people- connect people- aware people but law cannot provide food- employment- shelter etc. and if without ensuring basic human needs or addressing root causes kill or punish people, the crime never be stopped rather it increased dangerously and they revolt, law severely failed including lost people's faith or its value or acceptance. On the other hand, if addressed root causes or provide human basic needs which lacks fundamental cause of crime, then the punishment would not require automatically.

So, law do own job and for other, there proper system or authority has for others, they must act rightly i.e. government. With a balanced- collective- cooperative measures can get a sustainable solution, excessive or wrong approach of any entity like punishment in the name of law can gave birth serious crime. So, the marginalized- obsessive- extreme demand of law as presumes law is the solution is defocusing other true and fundamental organs obligation i.e. government.

People should never manipulate and defocuses the main organs of resolving any issues, the governments. An illusionary- obsessive demand of law defocuses governments responsibility, law is not alone solution but government is the main component to resolve the issues, that shall be focused. If government not working properly, law completely nil [just some framed dumb words] even the greatest law ever; if government rightly works, there law does not need more. The demand of people must concern about the issue that any unnecessary- illusionary demand should not be defocused main organs i.e. government. A formal and regular system must developed that Government shall be held accountable and asked before convicting any citizen of state that why the state failed to build a citizen good? What is the state responsibility or liability and how long it is been fulfilled or failed? Why a citizen of state commits crime and for state actual failure why state should not be hanged or punished instead of or with citizen? Why state not being prosecuted same in accordance with each conviction of its citizen? Each and every country normally today always like in a war zone, police- prison- arrest- punishment- hanged, a huge common war base!

So, there must act together- collective to resolve any issues sustainably without unnecessary targeting to kill or punish in the name of law. For a sustainable solution, the collective mechanism shall be worked, there never required punishment in general. Law or government shall be targeted to ensure human dignity- human potentials- human conscience, never targeted to disgrace- punish- force which never ever worked in history. A society builds together that law or punishment in small amount may exist but it would never be required and aimed to prove once it is unnecessary.

Humans are not criminal in nature, crime is not enjoyable party in general, no one do crime happily, there must have some reasons, crime is not human job. If act together, law educate or regulate and address root causes under good governance, there no crime and no punishment required. A balance at least highest tried, not excessive or obsessive one and defocus others. If want solution, act must together in a balanced or middle manner, if not act together or balanced way and ultravirus- unnatural- killing machine operates, it never works according to common sense and human nature- never crime stops- everything will fail and destroy. There people must aware that should free from illusion or obsessive to law and focus on other main organ i.e. government. It is public duty to ensure act together in a balanced manner, no one defocus own through shifting own duty to others shoulder must be also checked by public. There public must choose the right government to address the root causes in a right way and targeted to once law would not require that peaceful environment establish; though the governments necessity always sustained, it absolute in nature and be aware of it. People busy with something optional and defocuses exclusive or absolute. For a lawless [punishing laws] world law and governments or people must act together. People be aware from different ways and first must decide to be aware, but common sense or conscience is the best, even writing this books targeted to aware people. People must ensure act together in a balanced manner and checked no one defocuses other, choose right government to address the root causes in a right way and build a lawless world.

A human dignity- human potentials- human consciences world made through act together that leads a true world- better world- natural world where the peace and justice would be a custom and culture, it is peoples world and people can made it better together in a reasonable or logical- simple way, the real world.

The nature and number of crimes and crisis increased such an alarming rate that it is hard to find anyway to control or solve it. There some ways out of law or courts try to find, people fear in law and courts, but it is not properly developed yet and in a limited area it tries. Humans are today not try to understand, get into depth- cooperate the issues, they seek instant revenge or punishment- save only own baseless interest, that circumstances creates in today's world. The faith or relations are not working today, an

WORDS: THE ABSOLUTE THEORY

intolerant and unkind world built. No laws or punishment handle the issues, an extreme materialistic race-imbalanced development occurred. As, humans ultimate nature is kindness- good- cooperative, they feel and regrets sometimes but surroundings forced to be surrendered on race. The illusion- manipulation- positive deceiving are the best mechanisms of today to run the world, human failed-defeat- helpless there.

In all the cases, there is going an unknown extreme black competition- an extreme to extreme speedy race-uncontrolled and unnecessary developments. Human beings lost in dark hole, forget instinct, can't find the light. There is no peace- no security- no happiness, people each and everyday feels bad- worst than ever, feel that the way they run or live is not their instinct. But, such extreme and uncontrollable system developed in the world that system never allows human issues today rather human have to adjust or accept the system. The dangerous system developed in all the cases, human beings constantly daily surrendered and compromised. Peoples try to out, find the better way but system today uncontrolled and not allowed that it dictates human beings where human beings failed to win over the system everyday. The world today built, people feared and terrified, this world people never want or expect- it is not people's world. Peoples bound or forced by the system where inhuman activities commonly increased. No one stand and question raise there, mostly unable as system kills them routinely. All the fundamental system and developments today rigorously detached and dictates human beings, in different names people try to adjust but adjust with wrong results death and disaster. Everyday peoples try to find own, they lost all the way.

Peoples just struggle to live in anyway, there is no dignity or no peace, things snatching one to another as much possible in anyway is played. Human forgets its instinct identity, human made system made human inhuman or like other animal, human branded today criminal- bad- brutish, no one try to justify the root but accept- adjust- compromise. Human just try to live under any straw even, just try to find any shelter, lost their own fundamental ability- to think and decide. Human runs and runs, sensibility and thinking ability has lost, chaotically demands one and other without proper understanding, just find the way- fail to stand strong enough. System made humans today, human surrendered and followed, humans failed to create new.

This is not human's world, at the end of the day humans does not own this world; they cried and tried to find something better but failed. Though world is for human, human are not today well in this world. There human unknown to human, human feared most human, human doubts human and it is not human's instinct or nature or first impulse. It is dangerous for the world that human hates and hostiled to the human. Adjusting with problems dictating humans today, generation to generation came innocently but system bound them adjusted by older forced to follow and make it more rough and unkind. Today, problems in such level that nothing can stop it or tough to be optimist, but adjust and accept in different names. Consequently, there criminals are the leaders, there going arms competition, killing competition in different forms, competition of inhumanity and enacting disgracing- punishing law and developed system [to support it] but result is new extreme crisis- intolerance- terrible human sufferings. For solution, there must stop and think, go in depth and understanding human instinct or potentials and necessity or human role, addressing root causes or human needs and law may help to educate people respecting human nature and dignity.

One of the fundamental systems to the mankind- legal system shall be checked- reviewed- reformed immediate [according to human nature or instinct and modern civilization] that understanding its ability and human nature- respecting human dignity- realizing human potentials under modern civilization. A country shall be targeted or set goal or aimed to minimize and civilize its law- decrease prison- addressing root causes of the crisis.

• • •

## A Critical Review on 'Concept of Law' and 21st Century

**Abstract:** Concept of law has been facing fundamental challenges on that very modern civilised (social and technological advancement) century, considerate before demanding and enacting this existing trends or forms of law. Each and every day different kinds of law enacted as its demand, demands of law increased but why, what actually laws doing? Law see to us, who see the laws? We just bring, have we been generally checked the law at all that is the law itself fit or not? The old brand goes it by names, if law demands solution, where is that? Or is the law itself sole solution of any issues at all? This idea or concept of law has been served or not? Why the law is, what law is doing actually and concepts of law is matched with its demands or purpose? When in a civilised society extremely demands more and more laws, what it refers? We claimed to be civilised, are we? Is the law itself civilised? Should we need more laws or more good governance? Is the demand of law often defocusing the main agenda? Shall we need much more law on that civilised age? Can we say it a civilised age? Can we say fear is law or fear is peace while fear is complete opposite? Should we try to move on with least laws? Are we fed or swallowed insult ourselves saying 'no way' which deeply detrimental at large? This chapter is not about 'what is law' (definition), is about 'why is law' (ideas) and question is more important than answer sometimes. If there is any issues or challenges, it should be resolved or admit and clear to the people about the contemporary limitations of law as law is the demand of society. The traditional (continuing) existing legal trend, the basic ideas or concepts of law has been reviewed here on that modern $21^{st}$ century. As a matter of social sciences, here presents some relevant and remarkable facts but not draw any final conclusion.

**Keywords:** Law, International Law, Demand, Modern, Legal Trend, Binding Force, Shows the Way.

### THREE (3) THEORIES

1. Law is the greatest insult to the human civilization.

According to Thomas Hobbes (1588–1679) [Father of Law], human in nature are solitary, poor, nasty, brutish and short, this state of nature is followed by the social contract. How relevant this 'state of nature' today?! The existing legal trends clearly refers that human beings are bad or poor or wrong by nature, they are not doing right and they cannot, they need law to force them or punish them or binds them to do that, force or fear is the way to deal with human. It further add if anywhere demands law, it means there something goes wrong; as law means punishment and binding force, if humans okay, they do right, why the law is, is there any necessity of law at all? The law or prison increased means humans are not good in instinct, they do wrong by nature, and enactment of law begin its journey by

## WORDS: THE ABSOLUTE THEORY

declaring that human beings are bad, are rough and wrong, so there is law required to stop them or bound to do them. Law is the modern spontaneous/wilful/voluntary slavery tools of human. And most of the laws are threatening or punishment based, even in a simple 'Notice' also add the punishment with the bold coloured word. What it refers actually, it is evident that humans are actually bad in nature, they must be controlled and binds by lots of means where one is law.

There Augustine's doctrine of 'original sin' or Hobbes 'state of nature' proclaimed that humans were born bad in nature, and philosophers such as Rousseau argued that people were born good, instinctively concerned with the welfare of others. The scientific studies provide compelling data allowing us to analyze human nature through the clear lens of science, carried out by a diverse group of researchers from Harvard and Yale. Whether human's automatic impulse—first instinct—is to act selfishly or cooperatively? The results suggest that human first impulse is to cooperate that humans are fundamentally "good" creatures, willing to give for the good of the group even when it comes at own personal expense. Today it is an established fact, consistent data and research distinctively proves it.

The world decides once that humans are beast- they must be beaten or punished- they are slave nature and law comes; still this punishment- slave oriented concepts of law goes on and on that concepts we the people stand and demand more and more laws; we recognize ourselves bad-beast and submit to bondage or chain. So, the law or prison is not definitely good sign for human, its birth by admitting or declaring that humans are bad, and we demand it. Law is the greatest insult to human civilizations. The question is-on that modern age, human beings are at all bad by nature or bad in instinct? If not so why this kind of law or if yes, is that kind of punishing or binding nature degrading law can or could be the sustainable solution of any issues at all? If not, why this kind of law? Is there need any reformation-revision?

The US President Ronald Reagan framed urban poor drug-addled, pathologically violent and welfare cheats as culture war; he exacerbated dehumanizing perceptions to every level of government on that population. The Anti-Drug Abuse Act of 1986, $1.7 billion legislation allocated $500 million to further militarize the country, $322 million for surveillance technology, sponsored for converting surplus federal buildings into prisons. If humans are branded with that label, they lost the environment to be good in nature and lost the opportunity to address the causes of their actions. The base is starts from a place of moral purity. Human might have some controllable weaknesses, not bad or evil. What we try to label "evil", is really illness, fear, desperation, hate or a combination. There hate and desperation have seeds in abuse, hopelessness, isolation, poverty and other injustices. Humans are open and dynamic for good and bad. So, Hate is also taught. But the nonviolence and empathy, the good can also be taught and put into action to eliminate these bad causes. Victor Hugo wrote in "Les Miserables" that If the soul is left in darkness, sins will be committed. Humans are not bad in nature; the guilty one is not he who commits the sin, but the one who causes the darkness. It is the darkness's the society what we form, and the leaders we give power to, causing?

2. Why the law is.

WORDS: THE ABSOLUTE THEORY

For what basic reason more and more laws enact, there has different scattered reason but ultimate for peace and happiness, where is this? The conflict and violence are currently on the rise, non-state actors such as political militias, criminal, international terrorist groups; the unresolved regional tensions, absent or failed state institutions, rule of law breakdown, illicit economic gain, the scarcity of resources and climate change, have become dominant drivers of conflict. In 2016, the world experienced more violent conflict than at any point in almost 30 years. In 2017, almost half a million people killed in homicides, 89,000 killed in active armed conflicts and the 19,000 killed in terrorist attacks. Countries in the Americas have the worst homicide rates by a wide margin, accounting for 37% of the global total in a region that accounts for only 13% of the world's population. In the past 15 years, Political violence becomes an unstoppable dangerous factor where more than half of the world's population has lived in direct contact or proximity to significant political violence. For women and girls, the home remains the most dangerous and unsafe place. Some 58% of female homicides were carried out by intimate partners or family members in 2017, up from 47% in 2012.

Is the world in peace or individual in happiness? The law served its purpose at all? Everyday law enacts, more and more law comes, there is not a single issue where law is not but what is the result, what is the outcome? Some temporary magical solution shows but ultimate no one get it demands/needs. Law told about justice, equality, equity; anybody of today can give the verdict on that case that justice is where?! The world is in a crucial phase, democracy in questioned, war goes on by different ways, hunger continues, discrimination on, and where is law?

The worlds 1.3 billion Population lives in multidimensional poverty, 644 million are children under age 18. About 269 million people used drugs worldwide in 2018 and it is increasing than past, over 35 million people suffer from drug use disorders. On Easter Sunday, 359 people killed and 500 injured in a terrorist attack at churches and top-end hotels across Sri Lanka. In 1970 to 2019, 170,000 terrorist incidents reported under Global Terrorism Database (GTD). More than 170 million people are unemployed and it is increasing. 464,000 people have been killed in intentional homicide in 2017. Though all the countries have extreme to extreme law i.e. most of capital punishment but it is on. Globally, an estimated 736 million women have been subjected to intimate partner violence, non-partner sexual violence, or both at least once in their life. Though most of the countries i.e. 155 more countries have laws on domestic violence, 140 countries have laws on sexual harassment in the workplace.

Poverty, unemployment, drugs etc. are the cause and crisis, not law anywhere. This fearing nature human disgracing legal system in some way rather facilitates the problems, not solution. Where world goes? In 1994, $30.2 billion's crime bill the Clinton's allocated $9.7 billion for new prison construction, $10.8 billion for additional 100,000 police officers on the streets and 10.6% Black unemployment rate in the country, the programs were funded by cutting 270,000 jobs. The 40-year project has made America the global leader in incarceration. There 8 million renters face eviction and homelessness, overdose (drugs) deaths 70,980 lives in 2019, 8 million Americans have been driven into poverty since May. The socioeconomic problems have heightened during the pandemic, but police and prisons cannot provide any

WORDS: THE ABSOLUTE THEORY

solution rather creates more instability and crisis in the country.

Is there any sustainable solution law can give at all? There law available, but solution is not; law told it comes to control but it cannot. So, why this traditional forms binding or penal law is? The question is- is the law at all solution of any issues? Is there law can give any sustainable solution of any issues? If not, so what is and why is? If law is just theory and theoretically right but problem in implementation mechanism, so law is not an independent entity, it's not the solution or can't fulfil/reach the solution? If it's not independent, are we concern about other true fundamental tools (i.e. good government or governance) to reach a sustainable solution as much as we concern about law like an independent mechanism i.e. too often we rush to the law- demand law for solutions to all problems that we face or judicial killing i.e. punishment is enough satisfactory, no matter what next day it (crime) repeats in a double? Extreme demands of law defocus the governance? Shouldn't we to be clear publicly about this law limitations and more balanced concern for real reasons? Or if implementation is the part of law, so law or existing legal system fails to its purpose, it cannot serve yet for what it comes? The world needs solution, where is that? So, is the law solution for any issues at all? If not, so what? If yes, where and how?

3. The promoters of law- academicians and judiciary.

They basically demands law more and more, they follow this existing trends without checking consistent and try to achieve the people's faith on it. And they conclude as law is the solution of all. Is the law an independent entity to resolve any issues? If yes, why the world is in such historic terrible trouble, what is role of law over there? If not, so law

32

for what and what it's contribution? Is that existing binding force trending law framework is fit for modern century or not? What is the specific role of law on this era? There is law in every case, but peace is not there. Law for what and what it's role? Where are the grounds to say the law is solution? Is the law can be an independent solution? There specialise research and resources are extremely inadequate, do not have answer, do not think out of the box, just follow the way and advertise law. Sometimes court itself admit law (punishment) helpless, can't do anything, law failed. In South Africa, we can enact more and more laws, increases extreme to extreme punishment, talk about frameworks or training manuals but all of this is already being done. Law alone is not the solution, the policies and laws are only as good as the people implementing them.

## ANOTHER THREE (3) THEORIES

1. International law is the most civilized and appropriate for the time.

International law mostly not binding or punishing or forcing- fearing nature, rather it shows the way and share the proper guideline with respect to the human dignity. Explain and find the way, share the issues. International law is the most civilized and appropriate for the time. It can be the sustainable solution if it can get proper focus and place. There is nothing can be guaranteed in this world, everyone can just share and tried. The message to be shared, make understand and fill other needs to reach the goal. World is about proper and continuous or uninterrupted transmission of messages. No one can control anything anybody rather it messed much, be violent.

Fear is the sensitive and influential emotion on human mind. It has long been claimed as pillar of religious authority and after that it turns to a more secular and claimed as tool of political authority endorsed by Thomas Hobbes, sets aside religion in his magisterial Leviathan. Today, in all spheres more or less fear is the dominant theme as such politics, journalism, academia etc. and it is fundamental factors in analyses of what happens when people are threatened. A study on criminology have concluded that fear is the root of all anger. The homicide case of David Berkowitz 1976 (New York City), the infamous Son of Sam serial killer, is a powerful example of violence driven by rage and underlying fear. Fear is the root cause of violence, driven by anger. However, the law notwithstanding, human emotions trump rationality, and no emotion is more powerful or motivating than fear. Fear can interrupt and impacts on human thinking and decision-making in negative ways results in susceptible to intense emotions, impulsive reactions, and unable to act appropriately. How can this solely fearing nature human disgracing existing legal trends give a solution or support to establish peace where fear is complete opposite?

Nothing is stopped by calling someone his/her names, it must reach and be friends to understand the issues. A positive- dignified- deliberate vibe of culture or sense should be created. Whatever it makes to control, it cannot; punishment or force never can control any human beings, not any beast also. And cannot build a total crimeless, can control or minimize, some must exist and need some for balance also. Government is the exclusively preventive organ, not punishing; government should be liable for any crime or minimum security threat rather than law demands more and should chose better government. Law is nothing but just text, choose the right person in government and government is the law in ultimate, good government is the good law and justice, not a text or draft. Without good government law is off, law coloured itself according to glass. So, it's all about find the root and shows the way which is in international law.

To change, human instinct goodness and potential must be understood, it is not mere a philosophical exercise. This fundamental understanding or conclusions directly affect on human views to the world, these views affects on election of leaders and leaders affect on laws under human live which results in or shows the dealings about violence and its root causes. Human owes instinct ability to break the cycles of violence near and within. There should be a belief and support on nonviolent intervention policies and politicians, the better outcome with addressing root causes and sustainable solution in a discussion, not label or brand someone evil and punish. The peaceful responses to violence can create the sustainable ripples of change that will ultimately lead to less collective suffering.

There also demand by lots of entities or agents the legal binding force but/though it is in debate till today. Some of decides that this is the world of fear- punishment- force as humans bad- beast, way to binding force; it is time to review on that age, humans are bad by nature at all? So, the legal framework of all local or international should be like only sharing- transmitting the message or guidelines uninterrupted, shows the way and reach the issues in a effective way, may minimum/not punishment- fear- binding force. Human lives in modern age, not barbaric era. Defund the police, a tricky but trendy slogan in America and Angela Davis warned once, that policing and prisons could magically disappear our social problems and that the government cannot afford to pay for large social welfare programs. It is long time abolitionist phrase, now another barbaric truth come out with that the police violence has

WORDS: THE ABSOLUTE THEORY

not been stopped even in such disastrous- uncontrollable endemic and keeps failing to ensure social need which leads ultimate a condolence through last minute tricky emergency legislation. The leaders or government most primed sectors are policing, prisons, militarism to "solve" the social needs today, while problems are such as homelessness, poverty and substance abuse. The moral stupidity that produces these outcomes is not today's issues, history's largest prison system or largest federal discretionary military expenditure is a long time history of America. Today, it shows devastatingly that the highest office is at once a symptom and a cause of our decay. These failings are our inheritance.

2. Law is not independent solution framework, it can't be.

Law is supporting entity and collection of principles. Law act with other activity i.e. to find issues, reach root of the issues, open dialogue or discussions, fulfil the needs and necessity, government etc. Someone here to do something for not knowing or understanding, someone doing something for money/material needs, someone doing something by surroundings or circumstances, but the most prioritized is not knowing or understanding. If humans have bad and good both part and get the good understanding, then it boosts. Humans are not bad, they have controllable weaknesses. A positive- dignified- deliberate vibe of culture or sense should be created. So, shows the way- reach the message- guide in a proper way. A human being might be wrong but he/she also be the right at best as human being. Human have the ability to make choices, a free will. Free will refers people may choose to bad and also people can choose to stop doing bad, doing good which human's first impulse. The more governments

36

and individuals should support and create good environment, reduce the conditions that cause the darkness in which violence breeds i.e. poverty, unemployment, drugs, religious intolerance, homophobia, systematic racism, bullying, xenophobia and wars etc.

So, law shows the way and others reasons to trouble resolve i.e. demand/necessity, that is the most civilised effective forms. Wrong is never something enjoyment, there always has reason; reach and shows the way, if someone gets his/her proper right, never do wrong generally. [Congenital crime is not includes here as exception as inhume- unreal- unnatural and mostly impossible to exist, if it is confirm where existing legal trends already failed and then we can try another better i.e. proper guideline or conceptual framework- dialogue under international law to shows the way to change thought as human brain or mind changeable- dynamic- contemplative or flexible takes good and bad both under circumstances as intent creates act within certain area, go and check the circumstances creates it; forcing- punishing- fearing makes more violent and killing is not sustainable solution in this regard which already proved. Finally, sometimes few things may choiceless where allow last as first.] And the stand for rights is not wrong at all. Without giving someone's rights, can someone create much fear or suppressed by using or misusing law but it never resolved and it blasts which history witnessed and alas! No one learn from the history is the greatest lesson of the history, result wrong repetition. Peace is a straight line, it is happiness together, collective measures by nature. You must be happy with all, you can't be alone; rise above together, not alone. If there makes contradiction that do not give but want to get, never it happens voluntarily; may temporary not ultimate in nature. So, where is about understanding, law shows the way and where is needs, government shall be fulfilled its first i.e. food, shelter, employment, entertainment, dignity etc. Law act as coordinate or organized all the issues, supporting the other entities to resolve together, it's collaborative and civilised as peace by nature. Demand of law is not solution, punishment is not conclusion.

Law is not a neutral tool, either facilitate change and progress or hinder it. Whether law cannot relate with context and connect or serve the interest of the society is still law? In case of all the problems, people too often rush to the law or demands law for solution without properly diagnosing problem and justify the ability or limits of the law. Undoubtedly, there should have certain framed minimum standard or principles, but the over-obsession with law is in question today. Law is not an independent solution framework, good governance is the ultimate tools to sustainable solution. Enacting more new laws and policies cannot resolve the issues, rather it defocuses sometimes the necessity of good governance which can truly leads to sustainable solution in ultimate.

3. Law for the human beings, not human beings for the law.

Whatever the law is it should respect human dignity, to degrade human being nothing is to achieve at all. All the things should be checked and reviewed before demand it or enact it. The things just continued, more and more it comes, but what it is, for what? So, the more understanding- human centric thoughts- more research expected as engaged or relevant stakeholders or entities. The existing legal trends should be reviewed and a collaborative civilised nature should be initiated for this age under international law framework and good governance.

For individual remedy may some binding or punishing laws should exist but gradually it should be minimised, strongly discouraged under the very law as contradicts human dignity or takes to hibernate replaced by preventive and positive governmental human culture. Punishment never a remedy for state or society, it may temporary individual condolence remedy culture. State should never be judicial (i.e. not killing or punishing machinery), it should always moral- cultural- customary- preventive and positive or civilised.

So, Who is human being? What law says about human being? Why the law is? Is law independent solution of any issues? Can the binding force be a sustainable solution at all, to force or fear or binds someone resolve the issues in ultimate? Should the law act as shows the way? All the local and international laws should not be punishing or forcing or fearing nature, it should be informing- explaining- sharing- guiding nature, not binds. Law cannot bind, it rather have some negative impact. The ultimate way is to share the message and reach with needs in a proper way. It is better to start a day with love and empathy, not hate and force; peace is not individual, it is collective and collaborative.

• • •

**Reference**

1. Thomas Hobbes, English Philosopher (1588-1679). Leviathan (1651). https://en.wikipedia.org/wiki/Social_contract (See the Sources)
2. Rand, D., Greene, J. & Nowak, M. Spontaneous giving and calculated greed. Nature 489, 427–430 (2012). https://doi.org/10.1038/nature11467

WORDS: THE ABSOLUTE THEORY

3. Adrian F. Ward, Doctoral Candidate, Department of Psychology, Harvard University. Scientists Probe Human Nature-- and Discover We Are Good, After All. Scientific American, Founded 1845, Oldest Continuously Published Magazine in the United States, 20 November 2012. https://www.scientificamerican.com/article/ scientists-probe-human-nature-and discover-we-are-good-after-all/

4. Dwayne David Paul, Director of the Collaborative Center for Justice, a Catholic Social Justice Organization Sponsored by Six Communities of Women Religious. Prisons and law enforcement are not solutions to our social problems. National Catholic Reporter, November 24, 2020. https://www.ncronline.org/news/opinion/ prisons-and-law-enforcement-are-not-solution-our-social-problems

5. David G. Allan, Editorial Director, CNN Features. Breaking news alert: People are Inherently Good, Nonviolent. CNN, December 11 2018.

6. United Nations. A New Era of Conflict and Violence, 2021.https://www.un.org/en/un75/new-era-conflict-and-violence

7. United Nations Development Programme (UNDP), Human Development Reports. Global Multidimensional Poverty Index (MPI), 2020. http://hdr.undp.org/en/ 2020-MPI

8. United Nations Office on Drugs and Crime (UNODC). World Drug Report, 2020.https://wdr.unodc.org/ wdr2020/index.html

9. Sri Lanka Attacks: What we know about the Easter Bombings. BBC News (Asia). 28 April 2019. https://www.bbc.com/news/world-asia-48010697

10. Institute for Economics & Peace (IEP). Global Terrorism Index 2020.
11. International Labour Organization (ILO). World Employment Social Outlook, 2019. https://www.ilo.org/wcmsp5/groups/public/---dgreports/---dcomm/---publ/documents/publication/wcms_670554.pdf
12. United Nations Office on Drugs and Crime (UNODC). Global Study on Homicide, 2019. https://www.unodc.org/unodc/en/data-and-analysis/global-study-on-homicide.html
13. UN WOMEN (2021). Facts and Figures: Ending Violence against Women. https://www.unwomen.org/en/what-we-do/ending-violence-against-women/facts-and-figures
14. Ibid at 4.
15. Syed Mahmud Hossain, Chief Justice, Supreme Court of Bangladesh, 2021. Jashim Rady case, The Daily Samakal reported (Daily Bengali Newspaper). 06th July 2021
16. Jameelah Omar, Senior lecturer, Public Law, University of Cape Town, specializing in criminal law and criminal procedure. Violence against women: the law is not the solution. Daily Maverick, September 6, 2019. https://www.dailymaverick.co.za/opinionista/2019-09-06-violence-against-women-law-is-not-the-solution/
17. George E. Marcus, Emeritus Professor of Political Science, Williams College. How Fear and Anger Impact Democracy. Social Science Research Council, an independent, international, non-profit organization, 21 May 2019. https://items.ssrc.org/democracy-papers/how-fear-and-anger-impact-democracy/

WORDS: THE ABSOLUTE THEORY

18. Scott A. Bonn, Criminology Professor, TV News Commentator, and Author. Fear-Based Anger Is the Primary Motive for Violence. Psychology Today, The world's largest mental health and behavioral science destination online, July 17 2017.https://www.psychologytoday.com/us/blog/ wicked-deeds/201707/fear-based-anger-is-the-primary-motive-violence

19. Louise Delagran (MA, Med), Writer and Researcher. Impact of Fear and Anxiety. The University of Minnesota, Earl E. Bakken Center for Spirituality & Healing.https://www.takingcharge.csh.umn.edu/ impact-fear-and-anxiety

20. David G. Allan, Editorial Director, CNN Features. Breaking news alert: People are Inherently Good, Nonviolent. CNN, December 11 2018. https://edition.cnn.com/2018/12/11/health/ nonviolence-good-wisdom-project/index.html

21. Dwayne David Paul, Director of the Collaborative Center for Justice, a Catholic social justice organization sponsored by six communities of religious women. Prisons and law enforcement are not solutions to our social problems. National Catholic Reporter, November 24, 2020. https://www.ncronline.org/news/opinion/ prisons-and-law-enforcement-are-not-solution-our-social-problems

22. David G. Allan, Editorial Director, CNN Features. Breaking news alert: People are Inherently Good, Nonviolent. CNN, December 11, 2018. https://edition.cnn.com/2018/12/11/health/ nonviolence-good-wisdom-project/index.html

23. Dr. Collins Odote, lecturer, University of Nairobi. Law isn't the Solution to all Problems. Business Daily

(Africa), November 30, 2020. https://www.businessdailyafrica.com/bd/opinion-analysis/columnists/law-is-not-the-solution-to-all-problems-3213358

CHAPTER II

# UN Sovereignty: Transformation for this Age [International Organizations (IO)]

Human beings have a natural life cycle, different needs and ways human have to maintain for living. One of the necessary way is mode of exchange, exchange for distinct own needs. There different mode of exchange were in the history and now, once the popular was- bartering that exchanged goods for goods or things to things according to own needs and ability. On the ahead of civilization there comes modern and easy or smooth mode of exchange – money. It was and is the integral part of human civilization, it has an vital role in the civilization. By the time, human civilization progress and in last century it progress utmost. In a race, the world progress in material things and here world sinked completely. Consequently, progress comes with lots of challenges as last progress happened in a immatured- unplanned- unfiltered or unpurified way and it takes lots of measures to face this as instant as temporary under without proper justification or investigation which has been practiced constantly.

The root crisis is this improper- instant measures creates new problems as it is itself problem but the world try to find alternative than go in root causes and just hide the problems but not solve, then again in race. As a result, this crisis gradually develops in such where it goes out of control. The world builds as an extreme materialistic- unkind- ignorant world where money act as Frankenstein.

44

Money is a necessity, not everything but today money is everything which seriously confronts human lives. Everything has its limit or necessity, for the lack of connecting human nature and potentials, money goes out of its ability, and it affect human potentials gross or severe.

Money has bad and good part but unchecked and improper moves the bad part dictates world. Human have the ability to destroy or decorate the world, humans are the leaders of the world, human have the limitless power but nature sets a standard for everything and a speed limit that genius or ability does not demand invent Atom Bomb, limitless power or potentials does not allow unjustified full use of it. It is no intellect, it is serious ignorance. Someone owes something but do not know its proper use, it is dangerous like fire in blind hand which regretfully proves today.

There only one way remains is a destructive accident where world stands today, the world is not well today though world is in highest peak of its materialistic progress in all the civilization. Where money is immaterial-unnecessary there also money is the yardstick today, money becomes ultimate and world in race, it cannot see the deep root causes of the crisis, instant cash is the measurement of everything.

So, money naturally just a mode of exchange, but on that extreme materialistic age money is not only just a necessity rather it is all. Without money nothing is to think or happen in today's world, genius sold and died everyday is common phenomenon today. The world is not well as before said but it is better to respect the existing tradition to counter or challenge for change the way and other accept the nature.

Though money is need for any action as natural mode of exchange but on that extreme materialistic age money is the fundamental- uncompromisable things to proceed any moves. It is an established fact today and impossible to ignore this by anyone- anything. The question is how and what ways money should collect and use? This liberty and choice humans have as it owes good and bad both.

Money does not have sense, people made it good or bad. People have the full authority or ability to made choice on it as it owes good- bad both nature, good choice can build better world and peace. It can be such supporting entity to help the world reach in its true goals. But, it is the things should decided by people, people have that exclusive authority on it.

On that stage of discussion touching the centre point that- For an ideology or religion or politics does not require money must which ultimate demands or aims is to propagate the ideas or thoughts, publicity or advocacy of thoughts is the basic or ultimate aims, does not need money direly. The things can proceed in a way, in a limited resource or minimum monetary support, money cannot affect much on such exclusive issues. It is the things to direct connects human mind or thoughts- thinking, if it reached and people accept, the purpose mostly accomplished and the other individual practice.

When this ideology- religion- politics comes into develop a system or organization or party or government which collective- sustainable- actionable, there money must- undeniable- uncompromisable tools. There no way to ignore the money, no alternative to money. If there flow of money is not available- adequate, financial independence lacks, the idea and system both will be collapsed soon devastatingly, even if it exist in any way- it just as death body which does not any value or acts. There money is compulsory, on that materialistic age it is absolute.

An organization is a collective and common measures, there different organs- actions- officials involved, the maintenance and movements are necessitate finance. It balanced- organize- develops concepts and its activities which aims to sustain. To run the organization there money is absolute necessity, a basic- minimum cash flow is uncompromisable. For only advocacy of any ideology money can be compromised, if it comes into a system or organization or government there money becomes absolute as it is collective measures which involves some maintenance and activities to run and sustain for the betterment.

After clarifying and accepting the necessity of money, there stands a question on- financial independence and dependence. Why someone funds for any system or organization or party or government? No one funds single penny for no reason, it shouldn't be also. If anyone shares a penny for any system, there must has an own interest, an interference came in a justified or unjustified way and system must accept as it is financed by him/her. He/she demands his/her thoughts to accept and implement or try to impose own thoughts, aims to serve own interest, control or interfere policies.

Consequently, organization lost its moral basis, ideological strength and instinct from where and why it born, and structural strength or founding values and fundamental programs severely affected. It just exists in frame which waits for collapse and put in grave. It never serve its aims or purpose for which it is made, it never works for which it develops, it never accomplish for what it is founded.

Naturally, any kind of dependency is a serious weakness for an individual itself, for an organization it is death bed. If it is financial dependence, it is dangerous and specially on that extreme materialistic age. At the child age or primary stage may have some minimum dependency , but by the age everything should be matured and independent, otherwise it would be suicidal- kills anything.

Dependency never be an aim for an organization, specially financial dependency which absolute necessity for this age. Only a donations based organization can never make an expected- sustainable solution or never effective supporting entity to solution, may some conventional activities do but no necessary change or impact or a revolution never can made. Organization must have or find way to be independent on its existential position at least if it wants to exist in its instinct. Dependency suicidal for individual, genocidal or destructive for organization.

Financial independence is the things to ensure accomplishment for all. The international organization must consider and international entities should support to be independent international organizations. The world needs independent organization to coordinate – cooperate- contribute for the actual common good, they must have freedom of choice to stand for right as their founding values, to attempt on root causes of the issues. It is a matter of serious concern that international organization faces recurrent financial problems, more busy to serve donors agenda than its founding purpose, becomes a managerial organ for some entities.

International organizations are inevitable, though people made country through broke the world, but its one world and here the big issues are global, there international organizations for peace is undeniable. It may founded by some but gradually it develops through all of contributions and becomes universal, the necessary inventions never be personal.

United Nations has today reached its mature stage through cooperation of all the countries, it is a common-universal resource, a global needs. Though philosophically and structurally it reached in its matured stage but financially it faces recurrent serious problems. It is unfortunate that such an international organization dependent for finance and corrupted by considering personal agenda of its donors. The world needs an independent- universal- pure peace place of faith to see the global issues in depth where UN still suited best but it needs freedom or independence.

Non-profit doesn't mean anti-money or money-free organization, money is more important there to serve collective interest. Money plays an existential role today, death or alive. In all the cases, money matters, specially any kind of organization. Non-profit should understand its true meaning that it does not work for any personal profit or private property matters, it is non-profit on its aims-purpose- works- outcomes but for all of these money or profit in any way must. It is not a business or company-corporate or commercial which purpose is to personal gain where non- profit is for collective/common interest. There one thing common is money but different in specialization of purpose or aims or works/programs. Business also serves some common interest in the name of CSR but it is not their aim, it is a secondary or optional thing just. In non-profit, non-profit works or common interest or welfare is the primary and ultimate aim/purpose, non-profit also dealt with money. And non-profit seriously understands the impact and necessity of money, necessity of financial independence, freedom of choice. So, it is not that non-profit is an anti-money or money-free organization.

But, traditionally such an environment creates that non-profit is money-free, they does not have any money issue, they don't need any earnings, they just expend and serve. Any earning of non-profit is like unchaste or corruption, in serious question. To serve- it must earn, without earning how can expend or from where? Donation is the only recognized way today for non-profit funds, but donations serve its own purpose, not non-profit's purpose. Donation is another's, why you kept your lives on another's control? Donation can be a primary necessity but constant gross dependence on donations creates existential crisis, kills moral base and donation has own limitless limitations, impossible to rely complete. It is mostly impossible to implement or do a good thing under donations or dependence, without proper freedom and minimum security. Donation is not a reliable source or solutions of any issues in case of money at least, rather it creates much problems and unnecessary interference or insecurities to hinder programs.

Money with non-profit is a matter of question or impure in today's world but it cannot move without money. A vibe creates that though it plays with money all the time but it will be ruin if it tries to earn or independent in finance. Consequently, it dies but not earns or relates to be independency mechanism, if tries then system or tradition will kill it also. It is complete and dangerous wrong. This contradictory and hypocritic myth should be addressed in proper way immediate.

Non-profit should have a profitable or profit maximizing or financial organ to serve the organization and its flagship programs at least, purpose or aim is to common- collective interest. The existence must be protected, basic things like aims or ideology uncompromisable, fundamental programs should never be in insecured or uncertain position, it must served by own way. That much strength or reserve or cash flow should have any organization aimed or targeted to collective interest. It should not live on another control at least. The efforts or goals should have an organization to be free on that case at least.

The financial organ must separate- independent- minor or necessary parts of non-profit, it's never too big to hide or shadowed core purposes of the organization, organization should never more busy on it. A balanced- middle way must exist or maintained, not extreme that money-free or monetary but a proper- necessary ways must adopt for the betterment. As, finance is obvious, takes way for necessarily and as finance is not aim, never sinked into it. A check and balance must require which at present also maintaining, develop better system for good, without highest efforts to live in the best don't leave it to another's control.

Undoubtedly, donation would always be a major force to deal any collective issues, donations have the ability to change big, donation is inevitable but not it be the source to organizations existence, not for serve its aim- objectives or ideology, should not for its fundamental programs. Donations should never affect a organizations existence, a organization should never depends on donations for its life, it must have that aim- efforts- ability to live own at least, run own, dignify own. A non-profit must have absolute strength of its existence- ideology- fundamental programs, that stable force it must should have. Along with that donation is the always a major force to big change.

## WORDS: THE ABSOLUTE THEORY

Furthermore, economy is the pillar of the world today, organization should have a strong economical organ for its own and global concern or issues, if it can manage contribute on global economy in a way for better future should proceed. It is a natural and real needs or demands. The UN has like WB, IMF etc. as specialized agency who are contributing to the global economy but UN claimed to be poor- faces recurrent financial crisis. UN takes extreme position that not take or tries or involve to financial independence move or initiatives, necessarily cried and dies but not involve earn for own though has lots options but UN not as it unchaste UN. It is ready to die but not try to be financially independent, planned to be weak-dependent- enjoy existential crisis. The ignorance or negligence on financial independence of UN of its stakeholders destroying the UN gradually. Such a well established international organization, world's most necessary international organization is in the way of death with WB, IMF etc.

Non-profit and international organization are not same, non-profit may one of the common minor feature of international organization but international organization is so expand- deep- larger in aims- programs- platforms to deal global issues efficiently. What international organization doing is immaterial, material is what can they do is in laboratory format, international organization is the key development to build/create a better world. According to human nature- dialogue is the absolute way of resolving issues, international organization is the best places to deal with this. The impact and necessity of international organization for this planet day by day increased and expected. International organization can and must play efficient role to save the world and builds a better world.

If non-profit any kind of organization necessitate or require financial independence under own independent financial organ, so how much important it is for an international organization! International organization or UN is already too late to adopt that concept which absolute necessity for international organization to exist and work smoothly. The globally important platform must have the strength of its own existence, a model balanced way of financial stability, uncompromising position for its ideology or aims and international organization like UN can do it easily- reasonably- efficiently.

One of the greatest failure of the modern civilization (1800- present) is failed to develop an balanced- coordinated- cooperative [financial system or] economic structure, the greatest invention of exchange mode- money today hostile to knowledge- peace- happiness- welfare- human potentials. The civilization failed to build a monetary environment that supportive to peace- happiness- welfare- human potentials and knowledge etc. Money associated with throttled peace- hanged happiness- dehumanized- destroy- invalidate knowledge. Money creates an illusion of happiness but it never feels in mind and sustained to anyone. A colourful decoration outside it did as magical as temporary, it never a partner to ensure peace and happiness in true sense inside in mind, it never touches human mind, it creates unnecessary needs and complexity to break and vanish the sense of human. Money never be a friends for peace, for brilliance, for welfare, it always opposite to it. Money is fear for peace, threat to brilliance, weakness to welfare. It never coordinates or balanced with peace and talents, it kills it.

An imbalanced- uncontrolled- coordination gaped market or economy the modern civilization developed.

## WORDS: THE ABSOLUTE THEORY

Money made as enemy, not friends for peace. Mankind mostly in extreme, not balanced in any moves; they do misuse- uncontrollable- unnecessary to most of the things like 'money'. They use it over, made it destructive, sold self and became slave, go the things uncontrolled. Human starts race to race, speed to speed, no time to stop and think, everything cash and instant, instant lost own one day. Human made money 'God' as called- money is the second god of the world, and then human blame money for trouble and destruction, they feared money which they made God by own, and vilify money. The human beings sold oneself to money, and later vilify the money, feared money; people made money bad partner, money could be good. But, human lives in all extreme- race, imbalanced- uncontrolled- misusing all the things.

The modern civilization teach only racing, it forgets to teach 'stop'. Human beings today one to one, extreme to extreme race, more to more speed; no one stop and think, no one knows where to stop, no one knows the standard of use of potentials but misuse and uncontrollable situation they made where they lost themselves.

The world today in huge black competition, win to lead and dictates others is aimed all, for gaining something they creates unnecessary race and speed that goes out of control which finally stop in accident. Money made as the standard of all, everything controlled by money, human becomes beast to money without money nothing is to happen. There is an unnecessary or misuse of money that uncontrolled today.

In this world, there has more resources than human needs but human beings develops such system where no control of oneself, no right distribution sense, they forget that if anyone owns the resources than minimum needs, it is not his/her, it just deposited and must be properly distribute it. The inequalities and discrimination breaks the limits of sky in this modern civilization. People misuse of resources, creates artificial inequalities, human suffered extreme. It is more important to know the right use than gain something. To invent atom is may knowledge, not to invent atom is the wisdom. Mankind in most cases extreme- imbalanced- uncontrolled moves takes, they slaved themselves and blame to false things.

In today's world, millions of people in hunger but money invest more on arms; billions of people deprived from basic needs i.e. food, education, treatment, shelter etc. but invest more on police- prison- military; there lots of own country's citizen suffered but they (country) busy and investing more money to defeat other country. Money used mostly to dehumanize the world, it is not used for peace and welfare of the mankind as necessary than war and win. Money is the tools to disrespect- dehumanize- destroy human world, a race- extreme unnecessary and uncontrollable race to live carried where no one knows the stoppage and the crisis constantly goes dangerous to dangerous.

Peoples made money bad tools, surrendered to money, human beings itself made money bad and then vilify the money, neither they picked nor skipped, just pain and sufferings increased which destroyed and killed the people and peace. In an extreme race, no one has time to find root cause, no time to stop and think, everyone sold to money and busy to worship as senseless. Consequently, problems increased, crisis terrified, human sufferings uncontrollable.

People made money destructive tools, binds to money race, money made standard for everything, an imbalanced- uncontrollable- extreme monetary environment or

## WORDS: THE ABSOLUTE THEORY

economic structure people developed which swallowed/ kills peace. It kills brilliant minds, not associated with welfare, not friends for peace. All the things measured by money, money is single necessity as mode of exchange which ability is too short or limits (Aukaat). There thoughts- arts- relations- cooperation- mind are fundamental to peace and happiness, today all things sold to money which made all fall in one to one extreme race.

Today, the ethics- principles- truth easily be sold or compromised to money, there is no human dignity or instinct, no life. The world is an about consume- compete or fight and feed the body, not mind. No one has time to fix that the peace not only in body, it is about mind; not only about fight- force- snatched others to deprive and create artificial inequalities or discrimination, it is about cooperation- coordination- collective living and resource management rightly. The mind runs people, thinking is the ultimate human ability, knowledge never be an sold item named products, this is the true foundation of life and the world. Today, everything lost own value, human itself lost in money who made it. The imbalanced- uncontrolled, ignorance to use of brain and brilliance is in high in that modern civilization. Just there add one to another colours to cover root cause of unhappiness, no one tries to find and fix it. They just join one to one races, peace never they get, never the world get, the trouble is increased alarmingly everyday. The reason- character- understanding of life swallowed full by money, money becomes fear and enemy to thoughts and ideas or brilliance, it just accept the thoughts for race in money.

The existence- movements of the world depends on completely human reason- understanding- cooperation, it is killed today by money. When anything kills human reason- just make fall in race to live like other animal, it amounts irreparable loss which last to destroy mankind. This single necessity today controlled or led human, it measures human brain and ability, it decides life and death. The human reason- understanding- cooperation lost in money, the unfortunate thing is it does not give peace or life complete, may supportive where it becomes all and absolute. When the life or peace needs, it only came through understanding- cooperation- connection/relations in complete, if these things human lost then no one is safe, how much money anyone has?

Money or any invention which if it be greater than human, it will only creates crisis to destroy and damages. Human have the limitless potentials, but it must be used in a proper way in a balanced manner. Mankind mostly misuse or unnecessary use of own ability, a balanced and proper thing is being lost. Money becomes today greater than human beings, money can do everything today, peoples struggling to live, not enjoying the life. The world develops may infrastructures- building- places but failed to develop mind- peace- happiness. The world is not in well today, individual not in happiness. The ultimate things has not been achieved that human dignity, human beings sold everyday in market in different forms. Money leads the world today, not human and money is not human. Money is not in own level or position today (Aukaat), when something does not belong in right position that excessive, then it will always dangerous to the world and mankind. Everything has an own standard or limit, it must be maintained where money breaks it badly. It is the people made the money powerful, it is such powerful that human defeats everyday to it.

## WORDS: THE ABSOLUTE THEORY

The unchecked or uncontrolled human dealings always gifted severe destruction to the mankind like Atom, but human never easily learn from the history. Still more money on arms- war- prison, civilization comes and go but people doing faults after faults and busy to prove that humans are the worst creation ever than all other animal though truth is human owes the ability and first impulse to be good, result is a dilemma that not human nor beast. Human creates the environment that danger and destroy to them, the [financial system or] economic structure of today's world is one of it. Already, the money and materialism massacred the world, dishonour and disrespect to the human life is in severe, peace and security or happiness commit suicide long time ago, just a few mask roaming in the world.

Money fear, hostile to peace, weakness to welfare; it is a serious concern for long time ago but the speed of race increased, the problems not solved and today it is out of control. Still mankind not stopped and fix the root, find the alternative and join the race to accident and death. A balanced- controllable- coordinated [financial system or] economic structure world can be developed, if it committed it can hold the money in its position or level. Otherwise, this destructive- terrible- inhuman world may exist but no life- no breath- no peace there be soon.

Money has an own position- instinct, it has an own necessity and it must be in own place. Then money will not be feared or weakness, it can help to peace, support good and great. The global economy should be rethink, the financial system- economic structure should be reviewed, the money-based environment must be in own level or limit and controllable.

Money should never grabs an ideology, truth never be sold, peace never be hinder for money. Money becomes partner of peace- truth- thoughts and ideas. The misuse and unnecessary or uncontrollable use of money must be concerned and global resources are not for one, it is for all, it shall be equally and equitably distribute under a sense of responsibility and brotherhood. The existing economy and extreme materialism should be checked and balanced with peace and human nature. A humanize- welfare- peaceful economy the world needs, today's economy must be replaced. Money for military, arms, war or police- prison or dictates- fight/compete to destroy should be considered to decrease in limit, as much as possible money for peace, money for human, money for brilliance and ethics should be introduced; such economy shall be developed and it is peoples who must decide.

The world's largest and most recognized international organization- the United Nations, specialized for international peace and security faces severe financial crisis as recurrent problem pointed by UN Secretary General. The United Nations bound to cut its fundamental programs, failed to pay the salary of the officials in time, afraid to close the UNGA Debate and close the door in permanent. The world's most one prestigious international organization faces constant financial problem and repeatedly want money from member states where different excuses the states shows including USA that asked why they alone paid such big portion. For peace and security, humanitarian projects, welfare issues, there is crisis of fund or money. A most known- reputed international organization literally begging for money, it's in existential dilemma. In this way, money becomes a fear, insecurity, a serious weakness of many organizations and

WORDS: THE ABSOLUTE THEORY

individuals. Money corrupts, but for want of money destroyed many organizations. The most powerful organization the United Nations knee down to beg for money which kills its moral stand, through this way many of organization and institutions in moribund today. No organization works properly, talks freely.

Money controls all the peace, peace is small things to money and money is powerful than peace. It becomes dangerous, out of control and accidental for the mankind. When such institution like UN faces severe financial crisis recurrently, it damage its structural strength and grossly affect its ideology or aims and objectives, then it is concerning that the worlds one of the greatest failure that it is failed to develop an balanced- connective- necessary economy. A materialistic uncontrollable Frankenstein it creates consciously or subconsciously where they fall in dark area and running in speed to speed but find no way of light but terrible death.

This human race should stop and think, bias and extreme thoughts to be reviewed, uncontrollable and unnecessary things to be stopped. Globally, the crisis increased alarmingly in a different colour, mysterious issues comes and attack, the new- intake problems daily rise and goes out of control. In this globalization and technological advancement era, problems more global than local. All the things connect and affect one another in different way, no one control this. The worlds run after run insanely race to race begins, injustice and inequalities extremely increased in different manner. The world is in last point today, it is in death bed, it is doing lots but results nothing out i.e. food after food takes but stomach never fill. A frightening- horrible condition created where no one is secured, everyone is in danger in a way.

60

There people must act together, it is peoples world, human must decide on root cause and give full efforts, we must to see back, stop and think to fix. Where the problems and crisis becomes complicated and uncontrollable more as global as increasing, United Nations is the greatest invention in the civilization to play a guiding role for the broken and accidental world. There must someone who freely at least speak some true words, words for peace, words for save and serve.

For own interest, global interest, the United Nations shall be exist freely, it already achieve people's faith, it must hold it. To guide this world there must be an international-independent entity, to show the right way there shall be an organization that most recognized, in this destructive world United Nations works for reconstruction- renaissance. All the institution in different way mostly death, wrongly used and UN also have some failure but still its achievement that people's faith.

But, to murder UN –will be the last pin to the coffin for the world, at least an organization shall be there to speak right and speak for peace. To suppress, to control, throttle UN is amounting irreparable loss for the modern civilization. It was an great invention or creation, today it is in experienced and matured age where the worlds need it again that world is in accidental crisis, the world must share free space to the UN, the world must give independence too, for own interest the world should be give sovereignty to UN for sustainable peace.

United Nations shall be operate freely, it must be financially independent. UN must take up the way to be financially independent, it should not be dependent more. At least, it must be able to run its offices and fundamental programs, the minimum capacity it must gain/achieve to make its foundation more strong and that much independent position it must have to never it falls in existential crisis as global crisis. It should not die or sold at least, it must live and free. That financial ability and flow of cash it must earn for itself and for the better world. For peace and security, for the humanity and welfare United Nations must owe minimum available resources to operate its fundamental programs and its offices. There shall be cooperate for the own interest, it is global necessity. There question is not what it did or doing because it was or is not in such position but as independent organization in future the question can put what it will do or what it can do.

UN structurally and philosophically matured and strong enough, but financial independence is not there and as finance is all today, the other strength does not work properly. With financial independence UN can play an historic role for the international peace and security.

The United Nations organizational structure is much developed, globally its network strongly and diversely built, its association and coordination agencies joined with fulfilment. The officials and staff of UN highly acclaimed and tested, qualified and brilliant, clean and professional. Though UN is not an corporate or company and there working not mere a job, it is a peace organization and peace is a collective obligation where the officials/staffs shall be kept in mind- connect- own peace, feel it is not a just lucrative job or career, a challenge to establish peace. There a UN just a career culture raised and it mostly attracts today. The staff should be ideologically- philosophically connect with UN, own the aims and objectives of UN, became a people's diplomat who connect the crisis in mind and feel as own and give best efforts to fix it. There a serious lacks that understanding UN or peace, a crisis of spirit and efficiency found in today's extreme materialistic world cases. UN is not an ordinary job, daily job, a serious statement reading administrative works; it is peace building mission, it is place of faith of mankind, it is millions of people's problem solving efforts. The failure of the United Nations is failed to mankind, billions peoples distress to death, world is in a devastating zone, that is why UN came once which repeats today. It is not the story, cheap gossip or philosophy joke; it is truth, it is true idea- concept- philosophy that builds the world, it must be clean and clear to a UN official first. UN is an ideology, UN is an emotion, UN is a feelings. UN is a faith that relies on something who thinks about world, who can do something for the world, who have the ability to resolve all the irresolvable- innumerable- deep crisis of the age. UN is 8 billion people, the hopes for the world, a faith and believes. United Nations words is the action, dialogue of the parties decision, programs are peace, sustainable peace and UN officials must feel it where gave its best- connective- necessary efforts at least. UN staff must ideologically or philosophically sound- connective for this human's world that foundation or centre of this world, all the solution ultimate lies in there.

United Nations structure strong- dynamic- matured, the scope of structure broad and diverse, it shall be utilized and worked in highest efforts. It must be think- connect- share the right and guide the good way for peace. Not only observe, it must speak and loud for the peace. The ability- authority- scope it has, the staff shall be concerned and utilized it and connect with crisis in root and tried. Only dialogue in right place at right time can solve most of severe crisis of the world, a follow-up and committed dialogue. For the dire worlds necessity, United Nations shall be more

# WORDS: THE ABSOLUTE THEORY

concerned- connective- certain, the innovation and efficiency shall be more ensured, just not a ordinary or regular job but a daily developed and followed for something advance. A regular- committed- connective dialogue on any issues can be resolved and a sustainable way-out, UN must freely- efficiently- deliberately acts there.

UN should not be a government's managerial or executive body, like government officials or any states foreign office; UN must propose and address necessary and immediate crisis, not only from state orders but UN deliberately should be proposed on immediate issues. For example, UN or UN Asian officials should or can play an meditative role in peaceful power transfer of Afghanistan but UN failed to respond in time, may observing or wait for state orders or request but a huge damage and humanitarian crisis occurred there. In many cases, UN can play vital role in a right and peaceful way, through a follow-up dialogue. UN structure has strongly developed, it has huge network, it is matured enough and broader scope covered but it must be utilized in a highest spirit and proper way, the best utilization of resources UN have can build a better world and UN officials should owe this spirit to establish peace under UN platform and its resources. The UN structure is truly capable and organized in proper manner [excluding UNSC, see the main article] to establish peace and security.

The United Nations philosophically or ideologically (aims- objectives) rightly framed- developed- appropriate for the time, the purpose and principles of UN, Its founding values and fundamental programs are universally acclaimed and recognized.

United Nations should not be forceful- fearful- powerful, it must be dialogue- discussion- directives, a guiding organizations towards peace. Under Security Council UN includes some forceful measures and it is threatening to peace- state sovereignty- people's faith on UN. This force or power is alarming, for any reasons an organization cannot interfere state sovereignty, cannot force apply on any sovereign state even in the name of peace and security. International law and organization shall be adjusted and absolutely respected state sovereignty, UN charter clarified it also. The UN platform should never misused for some states own interest and blame or burden carried out UN, the force never used by some specific state for own interest in the name of UN. Sovereignty is absolute freedom, absolute freedom includes right to life and die both, no interference allowed on any cases.

The international organization must works on its area or aspects i.e. basically dialogue oriented. Any international organization should not be binding or forcing mechanism, for whatever reason it never interfere any of sovereignty, it cannot allow any force or violence. The power or force is the matter of states or politics, international organization do peaceful measures and rely on it. Human does not have any guarantee of anything or not known to the future, human can only think and share, cannot do anything. This is an effort based world, not result based. Force is the instant results way which cannot make any sustainable solution, rather creates mass wrong and say sorry after killing millions of people in the name of peace which was actually own interest (under United Nations). United Nations should not be such unjustified- unnatural- unnecessary forces part in the name of UNSC. Everything comes from mind, world must connects with human mind and UN should proceed here for independent- regular- effective dialogue including other entities or measures, find root causes to propose sustainable solution.

International law and organization should never be forcing or binding mechanism or organ, for any reason should never attack or interfere on anyone's sovereignty, should never power base mechanism. International organization must work in its area, in a peaceful means and address root causes. There political interference on international organization is terribly increased, international organization also influenced and changed much in power exercising attempt or approaches. Politics and diplomacy does not owe today individual- instinct-dignified position, it mingled, messed and dictates.

Though UN purposes are rightly framed or documented but in practice as an organization UN deviated from its founding values and purpose. It is concerning that UN became an power exercising and highly politicizing club of some states, the force or power is never be an sustainable solution and UN must be in peaceful and sustainable moves. UN is a place of peace, it should not be place of fear or threat. In all the way, mankind takes extreme and temporary accidental way, the good things became worst forever and United Nations is the historical landmark invention for the modern civilization, it must hold it values and people's faith.

So, philosophically and structurally UN strong and matured enough to be free, but financially it is in severe crisis and not in right way the UN. For own interest there world must acts together to build a financially independent UN which constitutes a United Nations that sovereign for guiding the world towards peace and betterment of the world.

For the betterment of the world, for own interest, United Nations should be an sovereign- independent organization, a free- pure- universal place of peace, to guide the world for peace. The world should not kill all the institutions, should not make inefficient all the organizations, should not misuse all the platforms for own unjustified interest. There must be at least a minimum guiding organization in that terrible and horrific crisis age, something shall be say words for peace and give efforts for the peace exclusively. The world should be UN free and UN should be do financially independent by own independent way. An independent- effective- world organization specialized for international peace and security successfully carried out its purpose should be the United Nations, and it is we who can made it for ourselves, it is possible, not just a hope rather real and justified under UN sovereignty concept, we must act together for ourselves.

In Concluding, the world needs a free- pure- universal world organization for peace where UN suited best still, there UN must come up with its good will to be first financially independent and gradually a sovereign organization with philosophical and structural strength which it gained already. Proviso, it must/only works on its area, fundamentally it works on dialogue which its founding values, and dialogue is the absolute solution where world should rely with patients time for sustainable solution, will proves by UN. UN will never denied, it tries utmost or efforts to resolve.

• • •

• • •

• • •

## UN Sovereignty: The Economic, Structural and Philosophical Transformations for this Age

**Abstract:** Peace is not mere a job, its collective obligation. The ownership (own as instinct), philosophical sensibility and service (welfare in action as job and obligation) are the fundamental ways to hold it. United Nations (UN) is the specialised and established place of all that with official and legal recognition. A necessary team exclusively- officially concern for the global peace as job as obligation. The question is, whether UN executives are free to think or not at all? Whether UN secretariats are just employee and United Nations Security Council (UNSC) employer or CEO of a pure corporate house or not? Whether world's needs a free pure universal peace place of faith (reliance) or not? The findings of the Independent Inquiry Committee (IIC) into the oil-for-food program revealed stunning information on "the politicization of decision-making, the managerial weaknesses, the ethical lapses" that characterized UN administration of the program. 'Financial independence'- is the question of its (UN) existence today, naturally dependency is a sensitive weakness. Concept of organization and state are not same but Organization works sometime alternative to states, there UN existence inevitable. Politicians interfere in diplomatic process, politics and diplomacy supplemented but not dominated. Politics and diplomacy override each, politicians and diplomats interfere in each other's business. UN has been facing inherent and by choice gross crisis. Here comes the concept of "UN Sovereignty", UN is now reaching at the mature stage of human faith and expectations by the support of all specially politicians; this is the time to be its own for the betterment of the world. So, Financial independency and concept of 'UN Sovereignty' is the main discourse of this study along with dialogue and UN's position on it.

**Keywords:** United Nations, Sovereignty, Dialogue, Finance, Dependent, Independent, Power.

## INTRODUCTION

UN sovereignty refers absolute authority to determine its own internal and external issues without intervention of any source's i.e. state, organizations etc. outside the executive body of UN (Secretariats). The economic, structural and philosophical absolute authority and freedom. Proviso, it exclusively works on its core purpose i.e. dialogue with its full efforts and limitations. Here (World) dialogue is the only solutions of any issues. This is an effort based world not result based where nothing can be guaranteed and anyone or anything can gave its possible highest efforts, not guarantee of any results. UN trying to be a forcing or punishing agency, powerful and fearful organizations under UNSC, not faithful or helpful. UN trying to be politicians or political organization, interfere in politics or exercise power. Power (i.e. any kind of force- contradicts itself under Article 2(4) of UN Charter) is politicians or state matters, UN may share its opinion if necessary. Power come back soon to dialogue, UN should be there.

Dialogue is the fundamental structure of UN, the United Nations itself was created in the belief that dialogue can triumph over discord. [Kofi Annan, Former Secretary-General, UN] The Organization is meant to be "the natural home of dialogue among civilizations; the forum where such dialogue can flourish and bear fruit in every field of human endeavour." In the context of diminishing resources, rising inequalities and shifting demographics, dialogue remains central. United Nations must uphold its founding values, build through innovative dialogue approaches. There is no peace can be lasting and no prosperity can be secure, without regular dialogue among all the nations of civilizations, cultures and groups. Accordingly, it is a reality of our daily lives that there authentic dialogue among cultures and civilizations is a obvious need. UN mostly deviated, just follows its daily jobs and choose the different way- emphasize on binding force i.e. UNSC (Chapter VII), United Nations General Assembly (UNGA) [A/RES/377 A, 3 November 1950] etc.

**ISSUES**

UN is structurally (Secretariat) and philosophically (Objectives and Purpose) strong enough or developed enough, now it's to be free to hold it up to make it better and efficient more as demand of time. UN is now in its matured age after a long way, it's ready to take its own leadership on that peace journey. The core issue is- "financial dependency" or inability, economic freedom is not there which now comes into begging. It is a crisis of existence. Standing on that crucial phase, UN totally controlled like as hired agency as finance is on another's hand. It must take into consideration of donor's special agenda, big donor- small donor, UN busy on that issue to satisfy them instead of peace as financed by others.

In 1981, the newly elect US President Ronald Reagan turned for advice to the Heritage Foundation who advised that the US reassert its control over the UN, either by holding back funding, on condition of certain UN "reforms," or by simply refusing to pay for objectionable programs and it was followed. It is all about money or finance. On December 31, 1995, the debts were totalled $2.3 billion and may be forced to close its doors in just a few months. In 2019, yet the Organization is facing a severe financial crisis, a severe liquidity crisis. UN badly reported, Our work and our reforms are at risk. The Secretary-General noted that this is a recurrent problem that severely hampers the Secretariat's ability to fulfil its obligations to the people we serve. Constantly, the UN has faced financial difficulties and it has been forced to cut back on important programs in all areas, even as new mandates have arisen. Many member states have not paid their full dues and have cut their donations to the UN's voluntary funds. Jürgen Stetten, Director of the New York Office of the Friedrich Ebert Foundation, Stetten pointed on the many UN member states unwillingness to take action to avoid a serious financial crisis at the UN, Quoting former British Prime Minister Margaret Thatcher, "I want my money back!". Though UN member states have been agreed to add many new tasks for the UN but without significantly increasing the budget. Mohammad Tal, First Secretary and Jordan's representative to the Fifth Committee, also observed same and he concluded that the UN needs a predictable level of resources to carry out its substantive activities.

Whatever UN has, it cannot use or work properly for its true purpose. As of July 2019, USSR and Russia vetoed 141 times, United States 83 times, UK 32 times, France 18 times, and China 14 times. Amnesty International claiming that these veto had used to "promote their political self-interest or geopolitical interest above the interest of protecting civilians." The organization suggested that a solution would involve the five permanent members surrendering their veto on issues of genocide. The veto has been marked as a threat to human rights. It is also anachronistic and unjust, the United Nations is meant to equally represent all its member states.

So, where is UN and what is doing UN actually, what should it to do or likely to do? U.S. President George W. Bush threaten to the UN in direct in February 2003 for their political self-interest on Iraqi provocations that free nations will not allow the UN to fade into history as an ineffective, irrelevant, debating society. In 2020, President Barack Obama repeated with same tone in his memoir A Promised Land that U.N. had stood idle in the Cold War, U.N.'s inability to tackle problems after Cold War, failed to reconstruct failing states like Somalia, or prevent ethnic slaughter in places like Sri Lanka. If the secretary-general takes any stand to protect civillians over political interest of any permanent members, the common accusations raise that he neglects his management duties and has installed a personal, untransparent regime; he has been too power-hungry in taking over political responsibilities; and he is incapable to reform the world organization. Thus, it creats an environment to call for an new secretary-general

There should be someone something at least exclusively or freely works for the peace without any intervention of any source where world can have a place of faith at the end of the day and there still UN suited best. Primarily, UN should be free from all this direct financial dependency or economic begging. The favour or clemency- direct dependency kills moral to stand against in nature. An international highly recognised organization depends on others for its finance, how disgrace and dangerous! Shouldn't have its own independent financial direct income source, how is it thinks or works or moves freely?!

**PROPOSED SUGGESITIONS (OTHERS)**

The most serious issues of the United Nations faces at present is its Financial reform. In March 1996, the Government of Japan presented its proposal on Financial

Reform to the High-level Open-ended Working Group on the Financial Situation of the United Nations. Japan emphasizes three points in its proposal- 1) the immediate issue of cash flow and the systemic issue of financial reforms should have a clear conceptual distinction. It is to be ensured that the Member States should fulfil their financial obligations under the Charter to deal with the problem of cash flow. 2) In order to achieve the reform of the United Nations as a whole in a balanced manner, the reform of the Security Council and the reform of the economic and social other areas should proceed together with financial reform. 3) The financial obligation to the Member states should be apportioned on the basis of principle of capacity to pay a concept that might be called "responsibility to pay," considering the special responsibilities and privileges of the Permanent Members of the Security Council.

The House of Representatives Committee, Parliament of Australia recommends in June 2001 that the Australian Government urge the United Nations to: 1) Develop more diversified and assured sources of income; 2) Set an incremental growth factor into its budgeting; and 3) Develop more effective penalties for the non payment of assessments.

In November 1991, Javier Pérez de Cuéllar, Fifth Secretary General of the United Nations urged the General Assembly to adopt the following set of proposals as elements of a 'viable and durable solution for both the short-term and the longer term':

- Charge interest on the amount of assessed contributions not paid on time;

WORDS: THE ABSOLUTE THEORY

- Suspend the Financial Regulations to permit the retention of budgetary surpluses;
- Authorize the Secretary-General to borrow commercially, should other sources of cash be inadequate.

Accordingly, he proposed for increase the Working Capital Fund; establish a temporary Peacekeeping Reserve Fund, a Humanitarian Revolving Fund, and a UN Peace Endowment Fund.

**REASONS AND RECOMMENDATIONS**

During his time as Secretary General, Kofi Annan tries to connect between the United Nations and the private sector, especially with transnational companies. There hundreds of agreements initiated for joint development projects and other initiatives between the UN and its agencies with private firms. One of significant was "Global Compact" between corporations and the UN. Hundreds of companies have signed on, but many NGOs criticised that the UN is compromising its integrity and providing a public relations cover for corporate malefactors. It is an example of simple- distant UN monetary organizational involvement in the UN history which not been worked successfully for some reasons and here some of advance answers. Undoubtedly, nothing is perfect or guaranteed and riskless but something has no alternative i.e. financial independency and here possibility high in some case as well as problems resolvable or risk can be managed too to better outcomes. So-

First, finance is not fear, finance is not a freak. Business or earn for own is not a forbidden things, a highly recognized and successful ways. Money does not necessarily means to be corrupts or personal interest

74

destroy the image. Rather now constantly, dependency corrupts and destroy in complete as abovementioned.

Second, there is no alternative to finance on that very extreme materialistic age, its common necessary tools of everything and there innumerable examples to best use of it which UN itself do already; just sources or ways should be change.

Third, as finance is must to do, the question is how can it be managed? Either independent- accountable or dependent- corrupts? Both options there, how many functions UN efficiently do! why not this financial management for its own and others?

Fourth, UN itself dealt with financial cases- reports on it- recommend on it, expert on it, why not for own? Which make it insecure to direct financial involvement for its own and others?

Fifth, it has world best recognized and specialised financial agency World Bank Group (WB) and International Monetary Fund (IMF), how can it be dependent for its finance to others?

Concluding, everything should be self-reliant by age, not to be depends on others forever, it calls disaster. Dependency is the crisis of existence.

### RECOMMENDATIONS

1. UN should have an own- independent- specialised financial management organ or income source may affiliated with WB and IMF.
2. Directly involve to earn for UN, UN should involve to direct income for its own administration at least as its existence.
3. Occasionally or programmes-project purpose (if requires) it may raise or share fund including

WORDS: THE ABSOLUTE THEORY

spontaneous donation but it should not be regular.

4. WB and IMF suited best to design and action plan as they highly recognized and expert on that very field, if necessary UN can ask for some other relevant sources especially self- financed organizations.

5. A popularly recognized example is- 'Social Business' concept by Professor Dr. Mohammed Yunus, Nobel Laureate and Founder, Grammen Bank, Bangladesh.

6. Dr. Mohammad Yunus marked as a charity dollar has only one life; a social business dollar can be invested over and over again. As any other business, it is self-sustainable; not dependent on donations or on private or public grants to survive and to operate unlike a conventional non-profit. Furthermore, funds in a social business are invested to increase and improve the business' operations on the field on an indefinite basis, where funds are spent only once on the field in a conventional non-profit.

7. The Second, BRAC (Bangladesh Rural Advancement committee) is the world's largest non- governmental non- profit international development organization, it is self- funded and donation based organization. It invests in social welfare enterprises or developments project such as education, banking, microfinance, housing, food, clothes and handicraft, seed and agro etc. It also a glaring and successful model for the world to be followed to financially independent organization.

Universal truth should be respected to do something better for this world as finance and financial independency is undeniable especially on this extreme materialistic age.

**STRUCTURAL AND PHILOSOPHICAL**

Dag Hammarskjöld, former secretary-general distinct two views on the world organization that either "as a static conference machinery" or "as a dynamic instrument of Governments". Kofi Annan, to the General Assembly, observed close that the current rules and regulations of UN were designed for an essentially static Secretariat i.e. act as a static conference machinery whose staff worked mainly at Headquarters. He further added, that is not the United Nations of today.

To amend UN charter,

- Make UN powerless or innecessitate the forceful power (any kind of force) i.e. UNSC (Chapter- VII) and UNGA (A/RES/377 A, 3 November 1950).
- 'Word' based effort or diplomacy (diplomatic dialogue) or "dialogue" should formally and literally include in the purpose of UN Charter.
- States be with UN as friends, not leaders.
- All the functions run by its own i.e. administration, appointment, activity etc.
- For the sake of global peace, UN should free- pure- universal.

Along with "financial independency" these amendments ensured "structural and philosophical" sovereign authority to UN secretariats as true basis of an organization, think and action room.

## CONCLUSION

With these measures UN would be a sovereign organization, works free and have the absolute right to try. UN be its own with philosophical sensibility as peace is not mere a job, collective obligation. This is the biggest challenges of time now.

"UN in diplomacy, UN under politics".

• • •

## Reference

1. Independent Inquiry Committee into the United Nations Oil-for-Food Programme, The Management of the United Nations Oil-For-Food Programme, vol. 1: The Report of the Committee, 1 September 2005, p. 4.
2. Secretary-General Kofi Annan quoted in Address by Koïchiro Matsuura on "Dialogue among Civilizations and Universal Values" on his visit to Peterhouse, University of Cambridge (2004).
3. United Nations General Assembly, Fifty-sixth session Agenda item 25 United Nations Year of Dialogue among Civilizations, A/56/523, November 2, 2001.
4. Ibid.
5. Hans d'Orville, Assistant Director-General for Strategic Planning, UNESCO. What the UN Can Do to Promote Dialogue among Civilizations. (http://www.un.org/en/chronicle/article)
6. Global Policy Forum, is an independent policy watchdog that monitors the work of the United Nations and scrutinizes global policymaking. UN Finance, Background& History, (https://archive.globalpolicy.org/finance/chronol/hist.htm)
7. Global Policy Forum, an independent policy watchdog that monitors the work of the United Nations and scrutinizes global policymaking. A Call for Action on the UN Financial Crisis, 16 January, 1996. https://archive.globalpolicy.org/finance/action/call.htm

8. Secretary-General's remarks to the Fifth Committee of the General Assembly on the Proposed Programme Budget for 2020 [as delivered], 08 October, 2019. (https://www.un.org/sg/en/content/sg/statement/2019-10-08/)
9. Statement attributable to the Spokesman for the Secretary-General on the regular budget, 08 October 2019. https://www.un.org/sg/en/content/sg/statement/2019-10-08/
10. Global Policy Forum, an independent policy watchdog that monitors the work of the United Nations and scrutinizes global policymaking. The Challenges of UN Finance, 22 March, 2006.https://archive.globalpolicy.org/component/content/article/132-links-and-resources/27324-the-challenges-of-un-finance.html
11. Ibid.
12. The Veto: UN Security Council Working Methods: Security Council Report". www.securitycouncilreport.org
13. Amnesty calls on UN powers to lose veto on genocide votes - BBC News", 25 February 2015.
14. Normand, Roger; Zaidi, Sarah (13 February 2003). Human Rights at the UN: The Political History of Universal Justice. Indiana University Press. p. 455. ISBN 978-0253000118. Archived from the original on 16 November 2020.
15. "UN failed to prevent 'ethnic slaughter in Sri Lanka' – Barack Obama". Tamil Guardian. 22 November 2020.
16. See, for example, Jesse Helms, "Saving the UN: A Challenge to the Next Secretary-General" Foreign Affairs 57, no. 5 (1996): 3-7, relating to Boutros Boutros Ghali.

WORDS: THE ABSOLUTE THEORY

17. Ministry of Foreign Affairs of Japan, https://www.mofa.go.jp/policy/un/pamph96/reform.html

18. https://www.aph.gov.au/parliamentary_business/committees/house_of_representatives_committees?url=jfadt/u_nations/unrptindx.htm (Australian Parliament House)

19. Yves Beigbeder; (1997). Adjunct Professor, Geneva, Switzerland. The Internal Management of United Nations Organizations: The Long Quest for Reform. Macmillan Press Ltd. p. 100. ISBN 978-1-349-13960-6.

20. Global Policy Forum, is an independent policy watchdog that monitors the work of the United Nations and scrutinizes global policymaking. , UN, and Business. ( https://archive.globalpolicy.org/reform/indxbiz.htm)

21. Social Business, Wikipedia, https://en.wikipedia.org/wiki/Social_business (See the Sources)

22. Dag Hammarskjöld, "Introduction to the Sixteenth Annual Report," in Andrew W. Cordier and Wilder Foote, eds., Public Papers of the Secretaries-General of the United Nations, vol. 5: Dag Hammarskjöld 1960-1961 (New York: Columbia University Press, 1975), p. 542. See also Manuel Fröhlich, "The Quest for a Political Philosophy of World Organization," in Sten Ask and Anna Mark-Jungkvist, eds., The Adventure of Peace: Dag Hammarskjlöd and the Future of the UN (New York: Palgrave, 2005), pp. 130-145.

23. UN Doc. SG/SM/10369, 7 March 2006.

# CHAPTER III

# Ideas of Politics: Socrates and Prophet Muhammad

The political ignorance is one of the key fundamental reasons for today's world and its crisis. It is made or created, different reasons exist but serious political ignorance is there in ultimate. The minimum understanding and efficient participation of citizens in politics, their impact in politics, their necessity in politics are the question raised by the time.

Human beings have the limitless potentials, each and every human being possess limitless potentials by birth. Everyone's owns such level of potentials than they needs, more than necessity. Every individuals have the ability to contribute or exchanged for the common good out of fulfilling own necessity. For some reasons, everyone's potentials may not be equally flourished, properly utilized, and used in good. But, the universal truth is everyone owns that much of ability than personal needs and it can contribute or exchanged for the better world. There also an established fact that everyone does not possess or expertise in all or same, there some diversity in common ability that some case something and some case everything or expertise of someone. There the needs of cooperation came, demands for exchanged one another according to needs and ability for own and others to build a better world.

It is more important to understand the proper use and utilization of potentials than just own. Individual have limitations, alone cannot fulfil all the needs and duties in complete. There in an alarming number of cases this potential misused, mismanaged and manipulates. Today, the owners of the limitless power who can contribute for the whole world, they are unable to live their own life happily or peacefully. They cannot manage their own life, struggling for live till to death. Hence, mankind made such a world where they live in a misery and death.

Individual develops a system named 'politics', for own interest and others, as human owes that much of ability to contribute for the world or common good out of own and everyone's single contribution can make the better world in collective, not alone. The purpose of the politics is personal and collective, it ensure the human needs and proper utilization of potentials in ultimate. Politics is a human made direct connected platform for the common good. It is a place of cooperation- coordination- action of individuals own needs and due potentials for collective needs.

A wrong concept kills the politics that politics is power; and so power tests morality, there most of the leaders in the history severely failed in different context. People lost their faith on politics, politics synonymous as nasty- bad things, people ignore and hate politics. Correction replaced in corruption, distance prolonging, politics and people illusionary differentiated in distinct class, the corruption and bad rooted in deep gradually. The result is today's politics, today's people, today's reinless world. Though politics is the known best way to do something good but people try to find alternative still.

Politics defined as power – force- instant magical solution mechanism, root cause or truth or effect of future or farsight or sustainability immaterial; a plce of forceful govern, imposing disgracing- disconnected- ignorant policies made by wrong authority, the peoples participation is just nominal or showcase, even in national or closely collective matters not place in referendum or plebiscite in the name of majority leadership representation which in nature highly possibility to be corrupts and it is established facts today but still no one seriously concerned. Politics becomes an ordinary job of specified class, it is only power issues, people lose their interest day to day. Gradually, politics goes and portrayed as bad things, lost its value and mass acceptance. People fear and ignore it, leaders manipulates and made it for a class though sometimes magic happens which is magic in actual. Regretfully, this manipulative power class deadly failed in their job constant, personally immoral and professionally ignorant or unskilled or wiseless, this so called power class severely failed in cases, politics becomes more hateful and idle things. Politics worse to worsen, planet faces daily devastation, manipulation and magician leads a world. People try to find the alternative way of better living where politics is the only way made and acknowledged or certified by the people.

Without checking and resolving the issues of politics, ignoring and losing in manipulation increasing human sufferings more. Where it is daily matter, it becomes seasonal only voting issue. People lost in race, try to solve any issues instant- temporary, don't find root causes. Politics is the place which they made and submit own all before politics, it is unchecked and day by day it becomes Frankenstein, bad peoples club. Though people try to stay away or manipulated by so-called politicians/leaders, but ultimately they must come in there and addressed as no way. Unfortunately it is too late to come back in there which daily issues, the damages happened and becomes uncoverable as long as people came there to address. The

WORDS: THE ABSOLUTE THEORY

sufferings increased, it becomes big and blast, a destruction occurred which pay uncountable terrific lose. The basic understanding and scope of politics is not clear to the people, not educated deeply about politics, that is the reason to happen this.

The danger is politics has defined as fight for power in anyway, peoples participation does not matter and people feels helpless there. Politics defined a force or instant-magical- populist solution mechanism without addressing root causes. Politics includes violence- fear- policing, it becomes synonymous to politics today. Politics is public matters, today it acts like complete separate from public. It is established definition and practice of politics at present all over the world.

The true politics is efforts for good- policy making or national character building- advocacy for public or common thoughts, to entertain people needs is the politics. The aim of the politics is not to only enforce, the primary aim of the politics is to ensure public participation, investigation or advocates and coordinates public ideas to frame as common goods. Politics is not only about govern, it is about dialogue- discussion- policy making and communicating to the public minds. Politics is not something to impose someone thoughts on public through force- fear- power.

People fear politics, try to keep away from politics, politics means fear and problems today. People does not own politics which engendered from peoples cock, it is a serious matter of concern and regrets. People disown and hate politics which constitutes a dark zone where mankind defeats and demise dangerously.

The political failure gave birth the non-profit or non-governmental organization as common, who doing this things most of because they feel politics is not fit for them, they fear politics, they think politics is only a place of fight for power. There is many countries where politics becomes an idle patronizing part of NGO, and shamelessly delivered speech that government cannot do everything alone though they specially appointed for this job, then they admit failure and amounts to individual lose in the name of alone where people pay tax and does not get service rather advice to do it yourself.

Politics is a power class, it includes force- fear- violence, a temporary- populist- instant solution mechanism without addressing root causes. Politics is not public matters, politics is not for all rather it specialize, politics is not about proposing thoughts rather imposing.

The astonishing fact is, human made system denying human, citizen pays taxes though/despite they disown, people made it and they feared. People forget in race sometimes, try to ignore the problems, feel it is not their matters but the ultimate truth is it is peoples made, people's problems, peoples matters and they cannot ignore this as they concern when problems affected severely. It is a daily matters, regular concern, voice for all agendas. There is no better alternative, it must be checked and resolved for the better. People made, people paid, peoples matters decides but people disown- ignore- feared, a deep and dark irony for the civilization. There decided a lot everyday about you but you are not communicated- connected- educated and suffered by blaming on wrong things- place- zones.

Everything is politics, politics does not belong special class or power, all the thoughts and works are the politics in a way. All the good thoughts and works serve the purpose of politics, politics is a name and way where good thoughts should be advocated and collectively implemented. It is a

## WORDS: THE ABSOLUTE THEORY

platform which made by people for own and others, as its purpose is to deal with people in direct, nothing is individual there and all includes in politics. What people think and do in the name of others except politics will be more efficient if it will be done in the name of politics or under politics. It is people's platform, it should be owned by people, used for good thought advocates and implements. Whatever peoples do they must require political recognition or support ultimate, politics is supervisory authority which made by people, so why people do not use own best and highest platform for good freely?

To disown or ignore this make a power class amounts to terrific and uncoverable lose every day, it is not only a power or governing issues, the basic of politics is to frame policy or to speak or advocates your thoughts. Government is made by people, it is bound to hear people and taking consideration to frame policy. Speaking is the human basic power, advocacy is the primary aim of politics, good thoughts when advocates and becomes common then framed policy for implementation that process named politics and organ named government. Politics is not something cosmos issue or critical philosophical science, it is public daily matters, politics is for all, it is paid by people, there people must respond on each and every state matters as state means people, voice is the key component of politics which all the citizens have and it must be raised.

Politics is the best way to good, it is the necessary place of public. It must be understood, utilized and communicated. Politics is not intellectuals or scientist matters, it is common matters, the base of politics is voice to raise, raising voice in right thing is politics. The power or development is not politics, it is a government which made by politics or peoples voice-vote. Politics or government is

86

not only a managerial works, it is public voice platform or places, their main job is to entertain public voice and public goods.

Politics is the place where human potentials can be utilized properly, there can get own interest and can contribute for others also. The contribution, its coordination- cooperation is inevitable for the better world. People must closely comes, claimed own interest and share contribution.

If politics is not in good moves, it is in wrong way, not commonly accessible or increase/apprehending, then it must be corrected immediate and return to its true purpose or origin. Otherwise, no one is safe until everyone is, for the sake of all, politics should think oneself- reviewed. People must aware, concern, initiate for a good politics, individuals need collective platform which named politics to government for utilizing human potentials and build a better world. It is necessary, if it is right then join or take part, if there is wrong then corrects it or find and establish a way as it requires. Before ignoring or hate something, there must a better invent or discover, it is better to light a candle than hate or curse the dark.

But, public participation, human potential, a better world is ultimate demand; mankind should decide for oneself, what kind of system and world they want or need. They have the ability and authority to decide on existing system and mechanisms. Politics matters, it is made by people but peoples are far away and feared today, it increased or continued and build worsen world that people suffered terribly.

The concept of politics and government is popularly corrupted- wrong- manipulative, it is a world of good and bad where politics possess and connects mostly in wrong.

WORDS: THE ABSOLUTE THEORY

The understanding and participation must be better for politics, it is simple and clear things which should not make complicated unnecessarily. With the passage of time, people in rat race on that extreme materialistic age where politics is hassle or trouble issues, only power matters, try to skip and no involve on such complications. Ultimate it affects and the sudden rise, but it is too late and results in disaster.

So, for a better world together all should build a political environment for more political participation, and for that the primary moves to clear the understanding of politics, concept of politics in simple words of clear thoughts.

There is no alternative or substitute of politics, before ignoring or after fearing something there shall be a better and new ways introduced. Otherwise, it creates a vacuum crisis which terribly destroys the civilization. A citizen can do own works which if connects politics that will results effective, if something going on as alternative to politics which completely depends on politics and it just a illusionary lie to mind for condolence. If politics is the system or way, whatever a citizen do, he or she first should be engaged or efficiently respond to politics, it is dangerous that in mind politics is optional where politics is all and must in real.

Without an established alternative, politics cannot be optional to any works or system. Where politics exist, it is the first priority and then other works may do as optional. Otherwise it constitutes the crisis that destroys the whole things. To ignore politics, takes any other way is just mere a self-deceiving things to do today many of doing in the world. A political environment should build to love it, connects or own it, deliberate respond on it.

88

The politics is not only for individual needs, it is for collective necessity or common needs. There put efforts not only for own, rather contribute for others according to potentials have. Each of one's contribution combinely or collectively builds a better world, not alone ones contribution or efforts. As politics for public or people, a common goods place, there human should share the limitless potentials for the benefit of larger interest, politics must offer such open and broad environment where human can comfortably gets such support to utilize his/her full potentials which can do better for this world. It is also duty of all to develop such politics or choose such politics which can establish or form an such government that promotes human-centric or human potentials utilization based policies and environment, it is the people to realize voice in politics to government for such environment and policies.

The another important thing is today people misunderstood politics and government that both same or government is politics i.e. politics means only fight for power. It is serious mistake or wrong, government is a one part of the politics, politics made the government. The purpose of politics is not power or government, it's common good or build national character. Politics is not fight for power, power is important but not everything to politics. Politics aims to advocates good or common thoughts, develop or own public opinion, to check the government. The main purpose of the politics is to share good thoughts connect with people thinking, brought some necessary changes in public thoughts for the better. Politics is the guiding way of good, identify the common good, from such environment to establish to entertain common good and encourage peoples participation. Advocacy of good or common thoughts is the core purpose or aims of politics which will or may from government or check the government. All the politics may government, all governments are not politics. People must participate in politics and check the government.

In this world, people cannot have any guarantees of anything, people can only think and share. People do not know the future, consequences but can try and share. The result is not in human hands, efforts are; this is an effort based world, not result based. To think, to speak and share is the best and primary efforts of a human. Politics is the platform made for fundamentally to raise voice- to think- to speak according to humans basic or natural or absolute ability, human must connect and share their thoughts- share their voice- propagate own ideas for a better country, better world which secure his/her and his/her sons future. The humans ability and aim of politics common for common good and thoughts, it must be utilized properly, it is peoples place and people should own it, connect it, change it.

Politics is the established and recognized platform for common good, it is human made, human paid for it. To find the alternative, it is better to find the root problems and corrects of an established platform. To this world there lots of platform developed for common purpose but politics is platform which is the leaders of all the platforms from the beginning to till. There lots of dogma came into politics, politics always aims to common good. There different forms of government came in the history, democracy is the best of all still today as it entertain common/public participation more, though without education democracy is dangerous.

Politics is the ancient developed platform for peoples need but with the passage of time politics faces different challenges at the modern time specially where technology has played a vital role, politics faces varieties challenges, there numerous ways to affect politics, good or bad both. It must make sure that politics must upgrade itself with the time as it is peoples places, it must act dynamic. But, it is a matter of concern that there lots of bad or manipulative machine or ways invent in the modern age which challenges every sector of the civilization including politics. There politics must be aware, people must concern, protects from bad and open for good. Politics is peoples place, made by people, peoples are the heart of politics, politics does not have anything except people. So, the challenges and problems of politics of today and before must be addressed by people, and own it, connect it, perform on it, raise the voice, respond regular, speak and advocates for good, common good.

The one theory or definition is- a common man place/ peoples platform/ humans stage.

Individual unites for common needs, it may form government or check the government.

Politics is an ideology, thought, common needs and on the basis of common good if constitute any party for advocating, it is political party. All the parties are not politics, all the politics are party or platform. Politics is a concept of common good, there parties form on that basis, party is not politics. Advocating for common good is politics, the party- power- government is formed on that basis, the basis is advocacy and common good. If any individual advocating any common good is the politics, not necessary to join or form a party, party- power- government is immaterial. Politics is a broader concept of common good, connects people.

WORDS: THE ABSOLUTE THEORY

To form a government or participation in election may require party but not necessarily always. It does not counter to politics i.e. advocating of any common good of an individual. An individual can be the leader or government chief without forming a party by the support of mass people on the basis of his/her ideology- thoughts-character which he/she advocates as common good and party or group may formed automatically.

So, advocating for common good is the politics, it may individual, it may join or newly established any party, may through questioning government, may propagating to the peoples aims to frame- develop- change or implement.

Speak- raise voice- speak or raise your voice for common good from your own position on own way, that is true politics. Don't just be silent, speak on common good for a world which you wants. Politics is about words, about voice, it is world of words, there's going on cold war or intellectual war long time. Hence, he/ she is the winner who possess more voice, silence can destroy the world, not bad or bomb or voice. Be aware, be concern, speak and raise voice at own for common good, it is your world. This is politics.

Only one condition for politics is- "common good". Common good and advocates for common good is politics. Common thoughts own but silent or secret, not open or propagate, is not politics. Politics is yours, you are the politics. Speak- raise voice- advocates for common good, don't just keep silent!

Voice for 'common good' is any form is politics. So, speak, don't just keep silent!

Politics not only power or govern, fear or force, is not violence and police- prison. Politics is peoples matters, common good, public places. It is made by people, people must check and contribute in its own way. Otherwise, something can happen wrong, as unchecked which affect people's severely. It is common-simple and absolute today to connect and speak for better world. Politics is in politics (bad), it must be checked and corrects- connects for change or common good.

Human is the centre of all in this world, human made system- politics to see the human affairs in direct, the most powerful and effective system of the civilization ever as it deals and made by the limitless potentials and highest powerful beings human. Human beings developed the system for human welfare, human needs and there human beings surrendered all the efforts. The world's best and fundamental creation, the leader of the world- human issue dealt by the politics. The purpose or subjects of the politics is only- human, politics means people, the human made only- specialized system to see the human matters. Consequently, politics is the supreme- sovereign- secured system or platform or institution of all, leader of all the way. The last and ultimate place of all, it controls or leads all the ways of mankind. Politics is the best way and most powerful system that runs the world, politics decide daily matters of the world, of the human beings, knowingly or unknowingly each and everyone includes politics.

Politics is made by people for people's needs, foundation of politics is to check the politics by people under their absolute- exclusive authority. To check and support the politics is more important than just accept and adjust. To know or understand and connect deeply with politics is existential demand of politics as human owns system or institution. The life of politics is human beings, without human beings it cannot exist or any gap between creates serious crisis. It is too alarming when creator tries to ignore

## WORDS: THE ABSOLUTE THEORY

or not take it seriously but under control. Peoples pay taxes, vote but just occasional obligation fill without further checking or justify the daily issue, mostly ignore or not taking seriously but adjust with it whatever happens. As a result, there gradually garbage grown, a dark zone developed, a bad blasts at last. When politics includes violence- hatred- corruption- conflict- negativity in extreme, people try to stay away and politics detached from public gradually. There is no one to check and politics day by day deviated from its purpose and takes wrong after wrong moves to be bad.

On that extreme materialistic age, all the things can be sold or bought, no ethics- principles- ideology there today and people fall in extreme materialistic race. The distance between public and politics gradually increased, manipulation and misunderstanding grown in politics at a higher rate. Politics becomes a dangerous tool for the world, people deliberately never engaged with it.

As in ultimate, politics is human made human affairs management system, it deeply influences human. All the important or necessary decision or policy framed in politics relating to public, it controls all the system or institutions, if politics is bad then everything is bad and the citizen impossible to ignore impact of that. Politics constantly right or wrong doing in public matters, politics creates environment and develop system that citizen consciously or subconsciously followed. There is no way to be free from politics, politics made people for own cause. The politics you approve, you surrendered all the things, it regulates or controls your external and internal behaviour in direct and indirect different ways. Only detachment or silence does not or never gives a politics free, everything in politics and in a way it influences citizens and it is concerning that people wants to be free from politics which they made.

So, the most powerful and specialized human welfare system if becomes bad and wrong moves, it is dangerous and worst than ever in history. When the best things become bad, then it becomes highest extreme level of worst in history. Today, the central or fundamental crisis of the world is political crisis- political ignorance- political misconceptions or misunderstanding. Politics deals human issues, it runs the world and when this way becomes corrupts then it amounts disaster. As politics is in centre of all system or institutions, most powerful and controller of all, mother of all organs, then politics kills or destroy all the way if politics is in wrong track. If politics does not work properly, politics acts worst than ever, there no system or institution works properly, all the way covered or killed by politics. If people stay away from politics, try to find other way and thinks okay, that is extreme terrific illusion ever. When politics wrong, everything is wrong, nothing can be good or efficient.

Where politics is in wrong way, there nothing can work, all the way becomes broken and ineffective. It kills all other ways, no system or institution can challenge it as powerful than other as human made human affairs dealings special-central system. As a result, there uncountable crisis happen every day, human sufferings increased uncontrollable, intake problems raised all the time but nothing can stop this, nothing works there efficiency, no initiatives or institution helps to out there, all the efforts severely failed, because political crisis or disease is not resolve yet. Where politics in crisis, without addressing it no issues to be solved by anyway. There such amount and level of crisis and sufferings daily happens but no system or institution

## WORDS: THE ABSOLUTE THEORY

or initiatives work there, it all destroyed by political virus. When the best becomes worst, it is such that history never before witnessed, and politics today in the way, world suffered.

It is serious misunderstanding of people today that subconsciously they just think politics is not all, it just a single organ or system like others, it is a independent and different system, it is bad and just stay out of it, just live own life. They cannot understand or forgets that politics is the place they made for all, a supreme authority they surrendered before all the things, mother of all system or organ. They cannot connect and understand its direct-indirect impact on human life, feel its complicated and not their issue. Politics is all, it is absolute, it is central or fundamental and human made it that powerful. Politics wrong means all the other ways also same in way, political crisis means mankind or humanitarian crisis, politics corrupts means the planet corrupts. Politics is not single/separate/independent entity, it is not individual or group; politics is all, it is supreme or absolute, mother of all the ways.

Politics is mankind, it is about people, politics is centre of all, it connects and deals all, it influences all. Politics is not separated or scattered or detached any institution, like other cases without addressing root causes find the alternative and thinks okay does not work in politics; there nothing can be worked, everything stopped or wrong moves takes. Politics connected everything in the world, without politics nothing can happen properly.

Consequently, the ultimate crisis of today's world is political crisis that political ignorance or misconceptions or misunderstanding, it is the root cause of all the problems, though lots of system or institutions developed but it cannot work because politics is not in good health. As long as politics not be checked and corrected properly, the problems and crisis never stopped rather it amounts extreme to extreme sufferings. There many good system or institution developed but it becomes partner of politics in ultimate.

Peoples try to be good, try to fix different issues but such political system developed there that no one can, forced to be part of political wrong. Without fixing political issues and checked regular, it is impossible to build a better life and better world. It is high time to think together about politics, political relations, political activity, political culture that fixes the root causes of the crisis. And politics is simple thing, it is not that complicated it made today or peoples think, the simple that- advocates for common good, sense of common good, attempt and aware, use words for common good i.e. speak for own interest and others, that is it. It is too late to be pessimist [HOME], if today not takes to correct politics, more serious problems or crisis raised that gave birth politics, billions of people suffered, ultimate unkind become one step closer to mankind extinct. It is established fact that, without politics nothing is to happen, everything under control of politics. So, without addressing politics, checking or correcting politics, no issues to be resolved and it is everyone's matter.

Everyday world faces more crises, unrest, different problems and the peace and security is constantly go far away. Nothing stop this problems, no ways worked there, no ways resolved the crisis; here politics is the one- effective- specialized way that can contribute and resolve the issues. Politics is public matters, politics can bring solution together, find the root causes and can fix it. Political coordination or political cooperation and proper understanding can build peaceful and secured world, no alternatives there. Politics can stop all the crisis, politics is people, it is peoples world and peoples have that ability or authority to decide about world. A good politics can give a better world and a better life. Politics is the ultimate place of all to resolve any issues sustainably and builds a better world. Without good politics there is no alternative to peace or to resolve this dangerous daily extreme crisis race, it is impossible to resolve any issues sustainably, just sufferings increased.

Politics born for good, its instinct or nature is common good, for a better world, politics came into force. Human negligence or ignorance for the time may develop it such a way that human fear politics today. The nature and purpose is to common good, human welfare, public affairs, if there right and regular efforts made it must get back to its own, it takes right and revised all the issues for common good. Politics is not born for bad or worst, it is made today but it is not politics instinct. Politics is the inevitable and absolute human necessity all the time, and it is human made for good, its instinct good or blood pure and fresh, so it shall be consciously and highly utilized for the common good. Human must return to politics, think about politics, check and corrects politics for the better world. Politics born for good, it is capable to deliver good, it can give a peaceful and secured world, a single theory for all the crisis.

There is a serious concern that- REALITY, it is highly used today to accept or adjust or compromise. What is reality? The things which peoples made for different reasons right or wrong, it is not natural or unchangeable mostly. People made something wrong, named it 'reality'- as said no way to accept or adjust or compromise with it rather corrects it or challenge it. In politics, it is mostly used by people to stay out of it that there is no way to accept it, it is reality though politics made by people. Nobody asks because people just need or find a reason to satisfy own faults or illusion or sense to stay away from something and here get the best used word without further study –'reality'. It is human made, changeable, a wrong but still used 'reality' tag and try to be partner with wrong or crisis in a cool manner. Accepting and adjusting with problems in different names rather addressing soon becomes uncontrolled and blasts. It is astonishing that peoples made something and people used 'reality' tag says no way, accept and suffered and deaths. The term 'reality' kills the sense, this misconceptions paralyzed human brain or potentials, it is murdered the human conscience subconsciously or consciously or over consciously. This illusion or self-deceiving or positive cheating ways are dangerous for the mankind. Gradually, it disown the world, disown the own made system, try to escape and escape from all the things but no way other than this world and human made system, a terrible results finally happened. It used like drugs to away from the world and issues but it is illusion and truth come out soon when no one can able to bear it, then a accident and close.

Human not concern for own world, not active with own made system, truth is the story or history and philosophy is the boring or unreal for today's people or world which in actual foundation and life or hearts of the world. A peculiar concept developed that in different tag's human divides and death from own world and system, they think that politics is only for a class and not them, to think about world is not their job and it is some other specific peoples job, a owner or creator of the things blaming and shifting which never happens but ultimate affects and unrecoverable damages occurred.

The world founding, the civilization build, the system to run the world born on/under philosophy- ideas, but today there is no time to think- understand philosophy of the planet or politics. Everyone in race and in anyway just fight and possessed more and consumed but at the end of the day cry for peace and happiness, blame different things that cannot find peace and happiness. There is no time to think and understand but cash or instant- race to race and the accident. The problems peoples made, crisis we creates and named 'reality' and many others, then followed, finally a beast's death and said reality is so cruel- terrible- upset.

Philosophy is the basis of life and the world, in market today thousands of ignorant approach happened in the name of knowledge but it never challenge the truth or conscience, philosophy. The true philosophy must be learn, learn philosophy of life, philosophy of politics, philosophy of world and civilization; philosophy is not a joke, its truth ultimate, it's all. Philosophy is real, so called made illusionary tag- 'reality' is not real or is fake and dangerous. This world born and made by philosophy, the ultimate foundation of life is philosophy. Before joining or starting race, learn how and where to stop, know the stoppage and think for next which answered can only philosophy. The peoples lost in self-made reality, and roaming under vicious cycle in whole life. Human in the early past few centuries mostly deviated from its instinct, they severely failed to manage their freedom and potentials, it extremely used in wrong way, lost in extreme- imbalance- materialistic race. They are effortlessly searching the peace and happiness through killing it by own hands, deviation from root but they searching them tirelessly. This civilization is the civilization of death, life is not exist there, in actual and symbolic. It is a destructive visible- invisible war between human to human, world to world, war to destroy each and same, all are confronting and rivalry in way.

Such a level of false concepts and manipulative things happen in the past century, it is tough to figure out where one is 'reality' tag. There is no reality exist, reality peoples create and crushed. For instance, there 10 foods for 10 people equally distributed, but one possessed other 6 foods by force or theft or techniques and this 'one' may waste it or enjoy it; now the 'one' pass the condolence [mockery] advice to others that this is 'reality', no way but accept- adjust- compromise, world is not so easy- there must face starvation and it is all about struggle, adjust it. There is no philosophy works- no ethics- no thoughts or words to challenge and corrects, just accept- adjust, this is the world. The astonishing fact is – once it did by kings or politicians or leaders, today they all relaxed and peoples itself do it with own and understand itself, the false and fake popularism developed where some advocates it also. Now, there no need to make people understand- the reality, they finely understand own and they just accept- adjust in the name of reality without further study and joking philosophy. Peoples may bit free from physical slavery, they chained them original slavery that mental slavery itself in different names and systems. It is made by you, why you not challenge or corrects it instead of named reality, why accept- adjust with wrong in different way? Today, human fear human, human is not well in human's world, humans are unknown to own world. Now, people blame the world and find the alternative without address root to escape but still failed, if finds an another alternative there also go people and problems in people, so same thing repeats as root is in wrong, where is the last?! Without addressing

WORDS: THE ABSOLUTE THEORY

the root causes when it constantly and commonly accept-adjust with the problems habituated, then it becomes big and high crisis, innumerable causes raised- life stuck into this bad cycle, it becomes once uncoverable and uncontrollable which results destruction- deaths- danger that today happens in many cases and human suffered much and loss. People made the problems such big that to give all the efforts even sacrificing life also cannot make it stop.

The world is amazing, it is beautiful and filled with available resources. It is the people must decide what and how they want to live, the world today built, there no one happy with it and peoples not getting peace or happiness in own world that they leads but nobody challenge as because fear and ignorance. It is human's world, human should own it, concern about its system and development. The misunderstanding or misconceptions should be addressed, the fundamental ability of human being is -to think should be properly spaced or used and respected, there is no alternative to think and learn philosophy and speak for own world and own system. It is terrific that leaves or ignore or excuse to stay away from own world and system in the name of wrong or false- fake varieties tag and concept; no way to escape from own, check- corrects- enjoy.

Politics is the ultimate platform to address the problems and all the human issues. It is the place to think and talk, there is no need to special membership to talk as it is made by people or own and inherently it owes all, connect-concern- advocates common good. It is too dangerous to ignore the mother system in different false tag i.e. reality or disintegrate own by identity, there is no alternative to it and in ultimate sufferings affects all knowingly or unknowingly. This civilization should more advance in philosophy-

102

concepts- knowledge, in social arena this civilization far behind than others. The basis or founding issues of the world shall be more advanced- studied- communicated- connected- practiced, the true knowledge- theory of understanding- conceptual development shall be made. A free- pure- universal ideas should be developed, connect with people, to enjoy the achievements of this civilization the philosophical or social conceptual development is must.

It is a regrets that the peoples are severely deprived from true knowledge- wisdom, true understanding- philosophy, the life –world. There false- fake- freaks possessed much in today's knowledge world, the knowledge or wisdom cannot develop and out from there. It is a 'war of wisdom' today where life is a joke and death is a celebration among same. On that extreme materialistic age, scientific imbalance race- falsifications regime, to builds a better, balanced and peaceful world, there is no way alternative to develop true understanding- reason- knowledge and wisdom, to connect and light people.

It is a political serious failure that people too believes in compromising today, accept and adjust is today's world principles. Nobody tries to go in depth and think, develop and challenge, corrects and create or innovate. All of in all cases 'compromise' instant, surrendered and slavery, no politics and no question. To free from slavery the politics born, this politics chained in mental slavery today, alas!

Accept- adjust- compromise kills the true politics, the greatest among people sacrifice their life and blood to build a true politics- born a country- build a nation with freedom and independence. Politics for freedom and conscience, it is not only accept and adjust, it is about human dignity and potentials. Today, peoples accept- compromise- escape from politics, politics itself in severe crisis today that came

WORDS: THE ABSOLUTE THEORY

to recover the human crisis. Peoples just surrendered to the system, no question or check, it is bad for politics, it affects politics. People must concern- question- challenges, develop true understanding- philosophy- knowledge- wisdom for the time. People must think and share the better understanding, in falsification people must aware and develop- share wisdom- knowledge, a living world should built, not only deaths. It is a great failure of the modern civilization that it is failed to develop a free- fair- good political culture, people extremely dissatisfied to politics, but the people must come across to deal with this issue to build something better.

Politics is the one- effective- specialized platform for common good- develops better understanding- knowledge and wisdom to think and share to public in direct. Politics is simple that to advocates for common good, it is human made system for addressing human words and needs. So, politics is public daily matters, it is better to connect- concern- check than ignore- stay away- hates. As long as, people connects- corrects, politics develop and better to build a better world. Politics is the human necessity, a fundamental- effective place of common good, it is peoples place and peoples made. To address the global crisis, political crisis itself first to be resolved, to connect- corrects politics is inevitable to build a better world, to develop better political education is necessary. It must own and properly utilized by people for common good, for a peaceful and secured world.

• • •

• • •

104

## "One, Effective and Specialised Way of Good is Politics: Socrates and Prophet Muhammad"

"Man is by nature a political animal: Aristotle"- [Man is by nature contemplative animal, and then political]

**Abstract:** Basic move's of good (welfare) is to call for good, cannot force or enforce and not guarantee of any results. Human greatest only ability is to think, sharing thoughts of good is the basic moves of good. Human have the exclusive and limitless power to think and share, but no guarantee of results and could not be real all the thinking but can share. In case of good, primarily individuals cannot force or enforce someone on something, can call or share thoughts or words. Good simply depends on individuals choice, others can only reach. If the ideas and thoughts became common between (or within) a group of people, they develops a system on common good, takes enforcement mechanism under system i.e. governance or government modern world named. The best good is to (make) think good, nothing can do more than that. No one can fulfil human needs, it is only can human itself. Others do one thing is to share the best way of good, try to build good in thinking or good thoughts. That good in thinking or good thoughts drives all the factors efficiently. For common cause, may follow some fix way where cooperation can be exchanged, if necessary. This is an effort-based world, not results-based, nothing can be guaranteed here. Here can think and share, gave full efforts to good but no guarantee of results, may not necessary also. Human can think-share, cannot do sure, may or not. To think and to share is the ultimate exclusive power of human, basic move's of good.

**Keywords:** Definition, Politics, Good, Power, Think and Share, Socrates, Prophet Muhammad.

## Definition

One and only purpose of politics is good, basic moves is to think and to share good thoughts, politics is about sharing policy, policy or good thoughts sharing exclusive or specialised effective platform. It is a complete wrong and unreal that politics is power, just a fantasy with dangerous moves. In the view of Socrates, the purpose of politics is not to capture power, nor it is an art how to remain in power. Politics and ethics connected in existence, political ethics is the highest virtue, it makes people good and proper citizen. Socrates practised politics, to shape moral landscape of the city through philosophy rather than electoral procedures. He was questioning the powerful members of Athenian society, brought contradictions to their belief or light. To guide people towards good and abstain from evil, is the politics in Islam. Islamic political ethics key base are the integrity, honesty, and trust. Politics is not mere about governing in Islam, it is fundamental tool for education, awareness, human understanding, spiritual and the dissemination of values and principles. Islam dealt with sincere advice, providing role models, rational persuasion, exemplary leadership and others. This is the way of politics in Islam taught and practised by 'Prophet Muhammad'.

Politics cannot give anything to anyone, just can share good thoughts, that is the core job of politics. For change, call to the change. To ensure material needs is optional or supporting and distant job of politics. Whatever peoples get from traditional politics (government), it is peoples resources, people can manage or arrange it itself, no need there politics. Core purpose of politics is to share good thoughts, shows the way, policy sharing is the politics. Here can find lots of ways to do same thing but it is not their only job or purpose, not specialised; in politics this is the exclusive or specialised only job, to share good thoughts or policy. To speak, to connect, to influence public in direct (directly) with good policy and thoughts is politics. Politics is about complete good, not partial. It is specialised only way of good, no other purpose. Socrates was a political artist, Socrates thought that he is the only one among contemporaries to take up the true political craft and practice the true politics. Socrates politics, was to teach citizen how to be good, why they should be loyal to the city and its traditions, to help the city flourish, deliver speeches to show the best way and guide the people in right. Socrates believes in correction than punishment, he thought that to teach true and sound argument is the only appropriate remedy for false and wicked teachings. He didn't hold any respect for traditional politicians and rhetorians under democracy who using tricks to mislead the public as in voting. Primarily, Prophet Muhammad invites individuals to his new revelation in secret for three years, very few supporters and believers have joined. Gradually, he started to invite more and more public, invited the elders and chiefs of the clan and then followers of the new religion started to grow.

Aristotle observed, the aim of the politics is to find good or bad issues to impact on government and to identify the factors favourable or unfavourable to the preservation of a constitution. Also asserts that all communities aim at some good, the highest kind of community aiming at the highest of goods such as Athens. Politician's fundamental tasks as role in a lawgiver (nomothetês) - to frame, to maintain, and necessary reforms of a constitution which involves enduring laws, customs, and institutions (including a system of moral education) for the citizens. Hannah Arendt

WORDS: THE ABSOLUTE THEORY

quoted Aristotle views that to be political meant that everything was decided through words and persuasion and not through violence.

After that, for larger interest, betterment of the society, for collective happiness develop a system under common good and participation with enforcement mechanisms i.e. governance or government or power named modern world. Building system to make the common goods effective, enforcing through collective measures, and public accept. Politics is the one and only specialised way where good is the only purpose by/through sharing to the public as thoughts and words to connect, to understand, to influence with hoping or high possibility to be enforced through collective measures or system as common good. To begin by saying and end with enforcement through a sustainable system, this is only in politics.

The new religion of Muhammad increasing gradually, attracted or joined more people and also increasing hostility with gross harassment and abuse. But, He preached and dealt with patience, resilience, and determination. The resistance to Muhammed and his followers were eventually forced them to emigrate from Mecca to Medina, a city 260 miles to the north in 622. This event called Hijra and marks as the beginning of the Muslim calendar. There Muhammad was not stopped rather became instrumental in bringing an end to a civil war raging amongst several of the city's tribes. This flight makes him more strong and committed to establish the Islamic community, strengthening the position of Islam, and spreading its message. In Medina, gradually gathering acceptance and more followers, Muhammad building Muslim community and settled in Medina. He lived in Medina for about ten years. In 632 CE, time of the

108

Muhammad departure or death, Islam had become a well established religion of the Arabian Peninsula and Muslims had become a major force to be reckoned with in the area. In 399 BC, Socrates also faced serious challenges, finally he was charged for corrupting youth and impiety by a jury of 500 male Athenian citizens (280 vs 220 votes). He was found guilty and commanded the death penalty. The followers urge him to escape but he spent his last day in prison refusing to escape.

Aristotle established his political theory in Politics book I that first, individual human beings combined for their natural or social need, build households for everyday needs and when several households combined emerged as village according to nature. Finally, for the sake of life, and exists for the sake of the good life, the complete community formed from several villages, is a city-state. Human beings are by nature political animals, and has equipped with speech to communicate moral concepts, Aristotle defends. There two political views are political moralism and political realism. Political realism is about exercise of power, political moralism is social function with a normative basis. Political moralists argued that politics is closely linked to ethics as such Hannah Arendt quoted Aristotle views that to be political meant that everything was decided through words and persuasion and not through violence; while Bernard Crick opined that politics is the way in which free societies are governed. Political realism represented by those such as Niccolò Machiavelli, Thomas Hobbes, and Harold Lasswell, politics is based on the use of power, irrespective of the ends being pursued. Politics is morally starts and ends through real, it combines both, though more scholars agreed that politics basically moral than real.

## EFFECTIVENESS

As good for human or public, people must connect or understand the issues or policies, human wilfully accept and develop system for change or good. Without direct human connection, understanding and acceptance, no change or good can be sustained in the long run. Politics is the effective ways of good as it direct connects public through thoughts or policy, it is the core job of politics. Socratic Method or method of elenchus (refutation) is about questioning or refuting on a specific subject or definition for searching the truth. Socrates participate in a dialogue with a known expert asking for a definition of the subject and he asks more question on that where the answers of the interlocutor shows inconsistency with his first definition, in conclusion proves wrong by detecting inconsistencies in his reasoning. In each round approaching truth even more or realizing the ignorance on the matter. Socrates also tests his own opinions, humbly acknowledging the man's ignorance while participating himself in searching the truth with his pupils and interlocutors.

The Constitution of Medina was drafted by the Islamic prophet Muhammad, a formal agreement between Muhammad and all of the significant tribes and families of Medina, including Muslims, Jews, Christians and Pagans. The fundamental concern was bringing to an end the conflict between Aws and Khazraj. It instituted a number of rights and responsibilities for the Muslim, Jewish, Christian and Pagan communities of Medina bringing them within the fold of one community. The Constitution established security, freedom, tax system, judicial system etc. Where human is in centre, takes collective moves, only specialised for good, there politics is in the supreme positions to work and control other all the moves or ways. In that case, can say that politics is power, all other ways to good dependent on politics as politics is (dealing's) public in direct. Politics is the enforcement or controlling or supervising mechanisms of all public policy or issues authorised or system develops by public. All other ways to good is not independent, not effective as dependent, not complete, not specialised.

So, one, effective and specialised way of good is politics.

**IMPORTANCE**

Other ways to good are supportive to good, but the best and complete ways of good is politics. Politics is the best choice for any good, it is must for today for own interest to closely connect with politics at least. Politics is public, politics is public policy, peoples are the authority to check the system they develop for themselves, otherwise something could happen unexpected. Politics not about power or leaders or a sum of peoples matters, it is common-collective- public. Politics for public, made by public, so no alternative to politics. No ways to escape if something wrong as part of system, it is Yours; takes the right action as politics, and no alternative works until wrong is not resolved in root.

Jean-Jacques Rousseau (1712–1778), outlined The Social Contract as the foundations of society based on the sovereignty of the 'general will' i.e. the power of all the citizens' collective interest. Rousseau believed that in order for the social contract to work, individuals must forfeit their rights to the whole so that such conditions were equal for all. "Each of us puts his person and all his power in common under the supreme direction of the general will; and in a body, we receive each member as an indivisible part of the whole." John Locke's believed that individuals

WORDS: THE ABSOLUTE THEORY

in a state of nature would be bound morally, by the Law of Nature, not to harm each other in their lives or possessions. To protect the lives, liberty, and property, individuals only would agree to form a state that would provide, in part, a "neutral judge". The citizens' delegation is the government's legitimacy as an impartial judge rather than each man acting as his own judge, jury, and executioner the condition in the state of nature.

Either connects or corrects, no ways to be silent or escape or skip as it is like Your body and parts where harms in ultimate. Politics made by public, put or sacrifice all things to there, and politics for good, do not harm Yourself by trying to be silent or escape, rather check and connect, according to Your authority. Good comes but be best bad, peoples have the exclusive authority to check, otherwise peoples will harm. Best things can be bad if it is ignored or silent on it, ignoring can fail the revolution. So, for common and personal good, connect with politics is must. Besides, others different ways can take (moves) according to ability and thoughts. The ultimate and best choice 'politics' should be always an important concern for public.

**Conclusion**

No one can ignore politics, pay the price in direct or indirect, on that context politics may absolute in some case, though peoples forget and suffered. Politics is public made best choices or ways of good, it should be properly taken care of by the exclusive authority 'public'. For complete good, politics is the one, effective and specialised way. Other ways are supportive or partial or limited. Politics is here in centre as peoples or human made as dealt with public policy or matters and public is the always centre of all ever. So, the best way of good and public have the authority or duty to check as common good. Some cases

112

politics is absolute, as much as connects with it and ensure better society, better world.

Therefore, politics is not power or leadership case, an effective and specialised way of good. Politics is public policy, policy or good thoughts sharing exclusive or specialised effective platform, daily life matters, public made ways of good and best way of any good, anyone's good.

• • •

**Reference**

1. Sunil Tanwar, Political Ideas of Socrates, Socrates: Life, Teaching's and Political Ideas, https://www.politicalsciencenotes.com/socrates/socrates-life-teachings-and-political-ideas/847
2. Johnson, Curtis (3 January 2013). "Socrates' political philosophy". In Nicholas D. Smith (ed.). The Bloomsbury Companion to Socrates. John Bussanich. A&C Black. p. 235. ISBN 978-1-4411-1284-2.
3. Dr Mohamed Azam Mohamed Adil, Associate Professor and Deputy CEO of the International Institute of Advanced Islamic Studies (IAIS) Malaysia. New Straits Times, an English- language newspaper published in Malaysia. April 27, 2018. https://www.nst.com.my/opinion/columnists/2018/04/362270/political-lessons-prophet-muhammad
4. Jack Miller Centre, An American non-profit organization and education Centre. Socratic Political Philosophy. https://jackmillercenter.org/cd-resources/socratic-political-philosophy/
5. Socrates, Socratic Philosophy of Politics. Wikipedia. https://en.wikipedia.org/wiki/

WORDS: THE ABSOLUTE THEORY

Socrates#Socratic_philosophy_of_politics (See the Sources)

6. Sayyid Muhammad Sadiq Al Shirazi. Chapter 1: A brief Biography of Prophet Muhammad. Al-Islam.org, a renowned non-profit organization to digitize and presents on the Internet quality Islamic resources. https://www.al-islam.org/prophet-muhammad-mercy-world-sayyid-muhammad-sadiq-al-shirazi/ chapter-1-brief-biography-prophet

7. Anthony J. P. Kenny, Pro-Vice-Chancellor, University of Oxford. Political Theory of Aristotle. Encyclopaedia Britannica. https://www.britannica.com/biography/ Aristotle/Political-theory

8. Stanford Encyclopaedia of Philosophy. Aristotle's Political Theory, Aristotle's View of Politics. Substantive Revision Nov7, 2017. https://plato.stanford.edu/ entries/aristotle-politics/index.html#supplement3

9. Leftwich, Adrian (2004). What is politics? : the activity and its study. Polity. ISBN 0-7456-3055-3. OCLC 1044115261

10. Greg Timmons. Muhammad Biography, The Prophet Muhammad. The Biography.com. April 2, 2014. https://www.biography.com/religious-figure/ muhammad

11. Louay Fatoohi. A short Biography of Prophet Muhammad. quranicstudies.com. Jan 29, 2004. http://www.quranicstudies.com/prophet-muhammad/ a-short-biography-of-prophet-muhammad/

12. Socrates, Trial of Socrates. Wikipedia. https://en.wikipedia.org/wiki/Socrates (See the Sources)

13. Stanford Encyclopaedia of Philosophy. Aristotle's Political Theory, Supplement: Political Naturalism.

Substantive Rivision Nov7, 2017. https://plato.stanford.edu/entries/aristotle-politics/supplement3.html
14. Politics, Moralism and Realism. Wikipedia. https://en.wikipedia.org/wiki/Politics#Moralism_and_realism (See the Sources)
15. Socrates, Socratic Method. Wikipedia. https://en.wikipedia.org/wiki/Socrates#Socratic_method (See the Sources
16. Political aspects of Islam, Islamic State of Medina. Wikipedia.
17. https://en.wikipedia.org/wiki/Political_aspects_of_Islam (See the Sources)
18. Social Contract, Jean-Jacques Rousseau (1712–1778). Wikipedia. https://en.wikipedia.org/wiki/Social_contract#Jean-Jacques_Rousseau's_Du_Contrat_social_(1762) (See the Sources.

Milton Keynes UK
Ingram Content Group UK Ltd.
UKHW010731070823
426447UK00001B/42